THE LAST
of
THE OLD WEST

A CAUTIONARY TALE

VINCENT R. LEE

sixpac
manco
publications

for my family
on a long, bumpy ride,
they've stuck with me
all the way

"Let this great wonder of nature remain as it now is. Do nothing to mar its grandeur, sublimity and loveliness. You cannot improve on it."

— TEDDY ROOSEVELT, GRANDY CANYON

CONTENTS

FOREWORD

I rolled into Jackson Hole in 1973 in an old Japanese pickup with a camper shell for sleeping in and an uncertain mechanical future for the truck. I came from the Texas coast, and was blown completely away by the Tetons and the valley beneath them. I never got to the town of Jackson on that trip except to buy gas, and only much later to Wilson, where Vince lived. "Give me men to match my mountains," someone wrote. Unknown to me at that time, Vince Lee was such a man.

The Wyoming of that time was a place of opportunity for people like me. A couple of years later, I got a job in Green River and moved to Wyoming full time. A couple of years after that and I was into Wyoming's environmental movement, stronger than many Wyoming people thought it was. Then I ran for and got a spot on the Green River City Council, then the legislature serving in both the House and Senate from Sweetwater County. It was a busy time.

Dominating the Wyoming legislature at that time were men who never saw a development project they didn't like. Coal, uranium, trona and oil and gas all maintained lobbyists in the capital at Cheyenne and all usually got most of what they wanted. One state government official, a candidate for a higher federal post, suggested in testimony to Congress that a new strip mine adjacent to Grand Teton National Park would be a good idea. It as a time of nearly wide-open exploitation of a landscape whose wild prairies, grasslands and mountains were seen by some to hold nothing more than mineral treasure.

Noted environmental author Barry Lopez describes the settling of the American West as a "ruthless, angry search for wealth." That is a good description of how it was in Wyoming in the time Vince describes. Lawyers lobbying the legislature were known to call members off the floor to dress them down for their positions. They freely bought legislators dinner and drinks. Politicians, myself included, soon became caricatures, easy to spot and pressure. Hustling the media, pontification, and redundant posturing of the most self-serving kind became the norm.

During those crazy years I wandered into Governor Ed Herschler's office in the Capitol one day on another matter and he asked me if I had any suggestions for nominees to the Environmental Quality Council. I didn't know Vince at the time, but a couple of fellow environmentalists that I knew had told me that he was "a good hand." So, I told the governor that I thought "that Vince Lee fellow from over in Jackson" was, uh, a good hand." Herschler appointed him and it was one of the best appointments he ever made.

There is a poignance and a thoughtfulness to Vince's reminiscences in this book that command attention. Those were "tumultuous times" in both Jackson Hole and Wyoming and Vince was equal to them.

Jack Pugh, Cheyenne, Wyoming
President, Wyoming Outdoor Council, 1979
Member, Green River City Council, 1980
Sweetwater County Representative, Wyoming House, 1981-2
Sweetwater County Senator, 1982-5

PREFACE

For thirty-four years, pretty much the middle half of my life, I designed houses for other people. I was a "small-town architect." That's in quotes because, for openers, there's really no such thing as a small-town architect. Nobody in a small town thinks they need one, or if they do, they can't afford one. If their builder wants plans at all, he's either got a kid in the back room who did OK in high school drafting class or he'll hire the guy down at the lumber yard with the same credentials. Then, too, the place where I worked, although certainly small by almost any standard, was anything but your garden-variety small-town.

But I've already gotten way ahead of myself. Even though I grew up within sight of New York city, ours was a semi-wild, wooded and sparsely settled neighborhood that, thinking back, set the tone of much of my future life. Named "Sleepy Hollow Manor," it was the setting of Washington Irving's classic legend of the 'Headless Horseman' and had once been the Hudson River Valley estate of John Charles Frémont, the famous and controversial 'Pathfinder of the West.' As if to enlarge on Irving's spooky theme, the explorer's abandoned Victorian-style 'haunted' house was right across the street from ours, and though strictly forbidden to do so, we kids nervously explored its dark and dusty recesses whenever we mustered the courage. It must have had an effect more powerful than I then realized, since like Frémont, I would years later be drawn, quite unintentionally, to the very same western mountains he pioneered, exploring their wilds and climbing peaks that still bear his name, when not designing often-empty mansions for the absentee Frémonts of my own time and place.

John Charles Frémont mansion, Sleepy Hollow Manor, NY -
Photo Unknown

Most of my boyhood, though, was spent in the woods playing 'Cowboys & Indians.' I always took the side of the Indians and still do. Sometimes, we played Robin Hood in old stone ruins on the nearby Rockefeller Estate. We even held up an aged John D. Jr. there one day and received a dime each for our bravado. While designing a house years later for John D. IVth, I was told we were the only ones that ever did that and got away with it. My dad worked in the city and took us there once in a while, but I knew early on I belonged outside, under the Sun. The only hint I might one day become an architect was that on rainy days I built castles and forts with my oak-wood blocks and Lincoln logs. They were defended and attacked by little lead soldiers and that might have been a tip-off that one day I'd also end up doing a tour with the Marines.

Fast forward twenty years, I'm out of the Corp, have an MFA in Architecture from Princeton and I'm married, with twin little boys. At this point, the story gets a little complicated as you'll see, but I'll cut to the chase: I needed a job and a place to live. With little thought about my professional future, I returned once again to the woods and picked a town so small it had only two paved streets and several hundred year-round residents. It was as far as you could get into the sticks and still be in the United States. A low-stakes version of the money economy had only just arrived there. Ugly billboards marred both road approaches over mountain passes often closed by avalanches during the six-month winter. The only other way in or out was through a canyon often blocked by both snow and landslides. Most people sheltered in leaky old log cabins or beat up house trailers heated with wood and lighted by a rat's nest of power lines draped all over town.

I loved it. No one cared who you were, where you'd come from or what school, if any, you'd gone to. To quote the Willie Nelson song, Red Headed Stranger, you were "judged by the look in your eye," and the locals gave you two winters before noticing you were even there. The only economically redeeming features I found were a tiny, rent-free log cabin for my family and a job with the only architect for hundreds of square miles. He was there on loan from a distant firm to design the base station for a new ski resort then being optimistically planned for the nearby slopes. I needed several years of apprentice-ship with him in order to qualify for a state-required licensing exam, somewhere down the road.

Thirty more years down that very road and my little town had become the hub of a world-class recreational beehive, with paved streets, Byzantine zoning, underground power lines, sign ordinances, leash laws and a hundred twenty-two busy architects, including me. The story of how that all happened is a good one I think you'll enjoy, but a cautionary one as well as you'll see. Lots of interesting people after me, passed the two-winter test and settled in. Some came to sell rubber tomahawks to the tourists while others turned ranches into subdivisions for them and the ever-increasing swell of skiers, the rich and famous and the service people that were needed to keep it all running. This last bunch was everybody from the lift operators and plumbers to the doctors, lawyers, architects and wannabes there hoping somehow to become rich and famous themselves. Did I mention lots of realtors?

Finally, there were the hippies. Well, not really, but that's what the others called them. They saw the peace, beauty and tranquility of the surrounding valley and adjacent wilderness going down the tubes. They were right and they fought it, thankfully with modest success. The result of all this was a town, valley really, full of interesting, active, highly motivated, over-educated, contentious and sometimes bored people looking for something to do. After months of dealing with right-wing ranch owners, left-wing tree huggers and everyone in between, a fancy San Francisco land-use planner hired to impose a semblance of order on it all, dubbed it a Rocky Mountain 'banana republic.' It was and still is quite a place. This is the story of the rise, and some would say fall, of Jackson Hole, Wyoming. Where did I fit in? I was part of every one of the above-mentioned groups but one, I never sold rubber tomahawks to the tourists.

Nowadays, my wife Nancy and I share a beautiful little horse ranch in the Four Corners country of southwestern Colorado, far from the "madding crowd." With a mild, two-month winter, it's a beautiful area and despite the fact that there's little not-to-like here, it remains sparsely populated. The nearest town of any size has fewer than 10,000 residents, employment opportunities being limited to the service needs of a farm-ranch economy I quit architecture when I left Jackson Hole and turned my practice there over to my third son, who came along some years after the twins. He's doing fine but, having played my small part in the utter transformation of Jackson Hole, I'm now happy to be putting up hay for Nancy's horses, overseeing our jointly owned business, designing barns pro-bono for my neighbors, and dabbling in pre-Columbian archaeology.

That's not to say I've given up on what architects care about or should at least: the quality of the world we build for ourselves. In recent years, gentrification has begun to creep ever-so-slowly into our high-desert world, historically a poor backwater in this otherwise fast-growing state. A few forward-looking new residents have even begun promoting a less hard-scrabble, more attractive image for the area. Curious, Nancy and I went to a meeting awhile back called to seek ideas for doing just that. Everyone was given red and green 'Post-it' stickers and asked to offer their thoughts on local problems and strengths, respectively. On my green sticker, I wrote: "This area is not sufficiently attractive to encourage lots of new residents." Reading my note, our leader said, "Oh, here's one on the wrong colored paper!" No, I meant it was a good thing.

CHAPTER I
"THE PLACE"

S pring of 1964 found me released from four years active duty in the Marines with a wife, two little toddlers and no job until the start of graduate school for architecture at Princeton in the fall. What to do? My final assignment in the Corps had been as a climbing instructor at the USMC Mountain Warfare Training Center high in the Sierra Nevada near Bridgeport, California. A British youth program called Outward Bound was just then getting rolling in the States. A new OB school in the Colorado Rockies near Aspen was looking for experienced mountaineers to staff its second season. I seemed to be exactly what they wanted, so I applied for a position, was accepted and hauled my little family up to their still-snowed-in camp above the tiny quarry town of Marble in the heart of the 14,000-foot Elk Range.

The chief Instructor was Paul Petzoldt, a crusty old Teton guide and veteran of the Army's famed 10th Mountain Division. His mixed reputation preceded him. A legendary 'mountain man,' he was nevertheless a controversial figure in some circles, having been involved in several high-profile flaps over the years. By the time of our meeting, that was all long in the past, but it was immediately clear that he did not suffer fools lightly and might easily have ruffled some feathers along the way. My military background, unusual at a time when many my age were trying to stay out of Vietnam, appealed to him and we struck it off well. My first job was 'patrol instructor' in charge of taking a bunch of teen-age kids through the month-long program. I enjoyed the work, but was hardly ever in camp, leaving my pretty young American-Swiss wife, Danielle, stranded in a snow-bound cabin with a pair of two-year-old kids. Not good. Things came to a head two months into the summer and Paul, hoping to ease the problem, appointed me head climbing instructor working mostly around camp, closer to home. It didn't work.

Famed Teton guide, Paul Petzoldt - Photo NOLS archives

By the end of July, Dani had finally had it and I agreed to skip the August course and get the hell out of there. Fatefully for us all, Petzoldt was also planning to bail, having become sick and tired of near-constant disagreements with the school's Director and his fancy, gourmet camp cook. Beyond that, Paul had discovered how few really qualified and experienced outdoor instructors were available to pursue Outward Bound's goals. He wanted to create his own school to address that very problem and was headed back to Wyoming in August to begin work. "Why not come on up to my place," he said when I told him we also were leaving. "Maybe you can help me get things going." When I reminded him of my grad school commitment, he said, "Come anyway. You might like Wyoming." Never having been there, Dani and I figured, what the hell, why not? We'd be together, at least, and out of what she'd come to call the "damned mountains" for a change. More on that later, but off we went to the rural town of Lander, nestled between the Wind River Mountains and the Wind River Indian Reservation, neither of which seemed likely to need a new architect anytime soon.

Aside from discussing Paul's many ideas for his new instructor training program, soon to be founded as the National Outdoor Leadership School, or NOLS, I got better acquainted with the man and his wife, Dolly. She ran the local radio station in Lander, and it was obvious they were well-connected in Wyoming. Dani and I took our time with them to rest up and get a feel for the state. Being easterners, we liked the wide-open feel of both the people and the land, but it hadn't yet grabbed us as The Place to settle down after grad school. That all changed one day when Paul, a bit impatiently said, "OK! If you don't like it here, take a ride over Togwotee Pass. If you don't like that, there's nothing out here for you!" We had a few days before heading east, so we loaded up the car with the twins and all our stuff and headed up the pass. It changed our lives.

Togwotee Pass divides the Wind River Mountains from the Absaroka Range as well as the vast, semi-desert plains of southeastern Wyoming from the mountainous, deeply forested northwest. Most of the latter is federally protected public land, most of it in National Forests or Parks, and much of it officially designated as Wilderness. 'It remains wild even today because the history of the region was largely that of the Rocky Mountain Fur Trade during the first half of the 19th Century, an episode that left few marks on the land. Prior to that, it had been the ancestral hunting grounds of several native American tribes and once the beaver played out and the trappers left, it largely escaped the deprivations of the logging and mining that so degraded large areas elsewhere in the Rockies. The result is an enormous tract of wild, unspoiled land, unmolested wildlife and spectacular scenery. Smack in the middle lies the valley of Jackson Hole, spread below the eastern escarpment of the iconic Teton Range, rising shear, without foothills, nearly a mile and a half into the sky.

Named by 18th-century French fur trappers for their resemblance to shapely female breasts, the Tetons, visible for many miles, had been important landmarks for early travelers in the region. Among these was an American trapper, Davey Jackson, exploring the Northern Rockies with the 1822 Ashley Expedition. Somewhere in the course of their wanderings, he gave his name to the valley that became 'Jackson's Hole.' We'd seen pictures of it all, of course, but neither of us had ever been there, so we approached the top of the pass excited to see what lay beyond. Disappointed at first that forest blocked the expected vista, we continued on down the far side hoping for better. Just as US Highways 26 & 287 turned sharply west, the highest peaks came suddenly into view, dominated by the 13,775 ft. Grand Teton. Still speckled with snow and ice despite the late season, they promised even more magnificent views as we continued down the pass. A mile or so further on revealed the entire range, towering abruptly above Jackson Lake and the forested upper valley. It was a spectacle beyond anything the pictures had promised! We were both stunned by the panorama and pulled onto the shoulder to take it all in.

The Teton Range viewed from Togwotee Pass - Photo Togwotee Mountain Lodge

For me, of course, the jagged Alpine crags instantly clinched the deal. They were exactly what I'd been looking for, epic climbs, with hardly a thought given to how a fledgling architect might make a living there. Dani instead focused on the beautiful green valley below and saw there the promise of a perfect home where we might one day settle and raise our boys. So right then and there, and for completely different reasons, it was decided: we had definitely found The Place. Just off the road, an old sign seemed to confirm our decision. Etched into some rough planks, the dark silhouette of a cowboy wearing a big Stetson, bandana and baggy chaps pointed west toward the valley and welcomed us to what it proclaimed to be the "Last of the Old West." Whether that was true, or even what it meant, we had no idea, but to our eastern eyes it was all we'd imagined our eventual home might be. Out of the car, a cool breeze brought the scent of pine and sage to us from the west, the only sound, the wind moving through the trees. After 20 minutes, not a single vehicle had passed us by.

Roadside welcome to Jackson Hole - Photo The Inn on the Creek

Continuing down the pass, the two-lane roadway cut into a steep sidehill and suddenly degenerated into a mass of cracks and dips due to what looked like the slow but inexorable creep of the whole mountainside down into a creek, raging far below. Our route being one of only three into or out of the valley, it was the first tip-off that access to our new-found Shangri-La was tenuous, at best, even in summer. Moving on and finally out on the flats, the highway dropped down alongside the now placid creek and followed it westward between recently cut hayfields scattered with cattle probably fresh down from summer pasture in the surrounding high country. Huge, fenced in haystacks and occasional 'beaver slides' testified to the old-time methods still in use. A cluster of tiny, log summer cabins alongside the road and a few old ranch buildings back in the dark timber were the first evidence we'd seen of any residents other than cows. Several miles further on, another rustic sign announced our entry into Grand Teton National Park. The ranch land gave way to sage and the mountain range began to take on something more like the classic form seen in the famous Ansel Adams photograph.

Grand Teton and nearby peaks viewed from Jackson Hole -
Photo National Park Service

Petzoldt had given me an introduction to his old guiding partner, Glenn Exum, who still ran a summer climbing concession out of Jenny Lake, hub of summer tourist activity inside the Park. Not knowing anyone else, we decided to look Exum up before continuing on into the town of Jackson at the far south end of the valley. Midway there, we turned west into the Park entrance at the tiny settlement of Moose. Not really a town, Moose was just a post office and a few tourist services, all appropriately rustic, along with the Park Visitor Center. A ranger there gave us directions to Exum's camp and off we went. The road to Jenny Lake took us closer and closer to the peaks and it became clear how big and tall they really were, the highest summits nearly 7000 feet over our heads.

Grand Teton seen from the road in - Photo All Trips

Glenn Exum happened to be out in the parking lot in front of the tiny Guide's Hut where tourists booked ascents of the Grand Teton, looming directly above. Assuming we were prospective clients at first, he responded more like an old friend once he read Paul's note. A few of his guides had just returned from the day's ascents, including several recently home from the successful 1963 American Mount Everest Expedition. He introduced us all around, presenting me as an equal among some of mountaineering's then most notable professionals. I knew it wasn't true but hoped one day it might be. Chatting with several of them, I congratulated them on their Everest climb and mentioned our intention to return to the valley once grad school was behind me. Glenn said there might be a huge new ski development to enjoy by the time I returned. Being quite the gentleman, as Petzoldt had led us to expect, Exum was also especially gracious to Dani, whose attentions were unfortunately also being sought by the twins, now awake in the car after the long drive from Lander. As she excused herself to deal with them, Glenn said he was sure one of his guides would be glad to take me up the "Grand," as they all called it, if I wanted. Boy, did I! We'd leave early the next morning, he said, and be back late the next day. Dani was still over at the car tending the twins, and when I told her of the offer, she looked me hard in the eye and said, "If you go up there, don't expect me and the kids to be waiting when you come down!" She was right, of course. After the lonely months she'd just endured in Colorado, I could hardly ask for more. I thanked Glenn for the offer, promising to take him up on it when I returned. He understood only too well, having dealt with marital stresses among his guides for years. As I was learning, mountaineering is seldom a good formula for marital bliss. We headed back east to Princeton and yet another life that same afternoon, not even continuing to town.

Princeton University - Photo by Denise Applewhite

CHAPTER 2

BACK OUT WEST

Fast forward three years and I'm coaxing our badly overloaded Volkswagen Squareback over the divide near where US 287 crosses from Colorado into Wyoming between Fort Collins and Laramie. I'm pulling a small U-Haul trailer filled with everything else we own, and the VW is hollering "uncle!" A pull-off at the crest to let it cool down brings the high plains of eastern Wyoming into view. A sign says, "Open Range. Watch for Loose Stock." Off to the north, there's hardly a fence post or power pole to be seen and closer by, melting drifts behind old snow fences up-wind of the road promise big winters ahead. I got out in a stiff west breeze and kissed the ground. It's early summer and the smell of sage is strong. Thank God I'm back out West where I belong! Off my knees and back in the now recovered VW, my first stop was Petzoldt's place in Lander, a couple of hundred miles further west. I hoped his offer of a job was still good, since I had no clue about work prospects in Jackson. Maybe I could jack up my dwindling bank account teaching climbing for a month or two and avoid showing up in Jackson Hole in the fall flat broke.

A lot had happened since that day at Jenny Lake. I'd completed the two-year MFA program at Princeton and been grudgingly awarded a Magna Cum Laude by a faculty that liked my master's thesis project despite our philosophical differences. Since my Princeton undergraduate days, before the Marines, the architecture program had morphed into a training ground for students of the then new "postmodern" movement. Its advocates, including many of my teachers, were mostly city people and devotees of early European modernists like the famous French-Swiss architect Le Corbusier. They viewed Nature as an abstraction, something pretty to be set aside and peered at through windows in little white boxes set on stilts as if to avoid getting their feet wet. To them, emerging 20th-century technologies were the new gods to be enshrined architecturally. Corbusier expressed the idea well: "The House is a Machine for Living." Really?

House, Le Corbusier - Photograph by Flickr user August Fischer

My years in the mountains had inclined me to share instead the alternative vision of the all-American iconoclast, Frank Lloyd Wright. Another controversial figure, both as architect and personage, he saw Nature as a womb to be snuggled against and embraced with a devotion bordering on reverence. His houses, especially, though strikingly modern in form, could seem both open to the elements and cave-like at the same time, burrowing into the Earth like an animal den fashioned from native wood and stone. Not only should we get our feet wet, he thought, but as muddy as possible, being part-time farmers working the land along with our other pursuits. His was an exurban world. The new technologies were to him just powerful tools for applying modern methods to the age-old imperatives of shelter, comfort and beauty. Best of all, I thought, his work was fresh and adventurous.

Iconic Edgar J. Kauffman house by Frank Lloyd Wright -
Photo Frank Lloyd Wright Foundation

With something like that in mind, I had chosen the design of a new Outward Bound School for my thesis project. Set in the shadow of Table Rock, a huge stone monolith back in the mountains of western North Carolina, it was to be a year-round operation. Needed was something more than the rustic summer camp facilities then in use by other, seasonal OB programs. The problem was how to provide it while disturbing the pristine natural site as little as possible. Road access was primitive and planned to stay that way. The whole point of the school was to challenge the kids, confront them with Nature and give them something more engaging to do than watching TV. The solution I came up with was akin to a sailing ship beached on a steep mountainside, but with a difference. The students would build the ship themselves, using small, easily transported, handled and assembled pieces. Tech would be kept to a minimum, with systems for heat, light, ventilation and shelter manned by the kids, like sailors trimming a tall-masted Clipper. That was the idea. The thesis jury loved it. The promoters of the school loved it. I was asked to go down to Asheville, the nearest town, and make it all happen.

North Carolina Outward Bound thesis project & truss detail -
Photos Vincent R. Lee

It was quite a coup for an unlicensed graduate with no experience in the field, but the school wisely put a local firm in charge of the project, with me in the back room drawing the plans. The professionals there also liked my ideas, but chipped away at them day after day, citing cost, building codes, construction practicalities, safety concerns, etc. until the project morphed into what I thought a plain-old building shaped to look like my clean, simple design. Worse, just as we finished a whole year of work, the Board decided to back-pedal to a summer-only program! Thanks a lot, but we won't be needing your year-round building after all. They had discovered what the other OB schools had already long-since learned: the only students available during the school year were delinquents and other truants uninterested in the program and only there if compelled by some sponsoring agency. It had been tried, found unworkable and abandoned. At the Board's request, I drew up a rustic, open-air kitchen/dining shelter before the project was closed down. We all got paid, but I was again out of a job and needing work. It wasn't all bad though. Dani and I were at last free to pursue the dream we'd agreed to coming off Togwotee Pass three years earlier. She and the boys went back up to New York, while I packed up our stuff and headed back out west to seek our fortunes. Petzoldt was glad to see me when I got to Lander but had already opened NOLS the previous year while I was in North Carolina. The second season was about to start, though, and he hired me on the spot. I already knew some of the other instructors, lured by Paul away from COBS, so my arrival was a bit of a homecoming. Again, I was leading patrols much like before, but this time with an assistant, Ben Giles. The work was good, except that the entire class trekked through the mountains together, 80 strong. Midway through the first course, Ben and I talked Paul into letting us work our patrol independently, a major improvement. We were allowed the same freedom during the second and third courses and we and our students made the most of it, wandering through the wilds, camping wherever we liked and climbing whatever we wanted. That summer became the foundation for an outdoor education program of my own that I was unwittingly destined to pursue for the next thirty years.

Best of all, we were getting to know the nearby Wind River Mountains. With hundreds of granite peaks and some of the largest glaciers south of Canada, it is the most alpine range in the American Rockies and a mountaineer's paradise. Nearly all of it is federally protected Wilderness, with few trails and even fewer people at the time. Truly magical country, the "Winds" remain my favorites even now, after decades of wandering many of the world's high places. As I write this, they remain largely uncrowded and wild despite the passage of time and growth of backcountry mountaineering. Except in the few climbing hot spots with easy access, trail approaches to the high peaks are still long, arduous and unappealing to new generations of climbers trained in gyms or on drive-up practice rocks requiring little or no trekking, load carrying or camping.

My NOLS patrol, Titcomb Basin, Wind River Mountains -
Photo Vincent R. Lee

September marked the end of the NOLS season and found me back on the road over the pass to Jackson Hole. Ben and I had agreed to meet there and do some climbing before he continued on to a new life in the Pacific Northwest, but now riding shotgun in the VW was my new sidekick, Mud. She was a Shepherd pup I'd picked up along the way getting gas at Fort Washakie, on the Wind River Indian Reservation, home to the Shoshone and Northern Arapaho Tribes. She'd just been run over by a pickup, but pushed into the soft, wet, unpaved station apron and was still kicking. I couldn't resist bringing her aboard. A quick stop with the Indian vet in Crowheart confirmed that "nothin' was broke," and she'd be OK. It was a good thing, since that little dog was to become a loyal and loving companion for my family and me over the years ahead. I'd been missing Dani and the boys after several months apart, and Mud had already begun taking away a lot of the loneliness.

My dog Mud - Photo Vincent R. Lee

My old Squareback, still struggling, finally made it over Togwotee Pass and the old "Last of the Old West" sign again pulled me over as it had three years earlier, almost to the day. The Tetons hadn't lost any of their mountaineering appeal and after my months in the nearby Winds, I thought the sign probably had it just about right. Continuing down to the valley, and on toward Jackson, my next stop, something unexpected and a bit jolting caught my eye just south of the Park boundary. A couple of summits left of the last of the high peaks, the slopes of what I later learned was Rendezvous Mountain were scored by rough road switchbacks up to what looked like several major construction sites. Huge, trussed-steel towers, painted rust-resistant orange, rose from each. I realized they must be the tram towers for the new ski area mentioned in passing three years earlier during our brief visit with Glenn Exum at Jenny Lake. With what now seems a bit of youthful naïveté, I thought, Wow! How cool!

Rendezvous Mountain, ski area under construction - Photo
Unknown

No cables were yet visible, but I soon learned that the promoters had promised to build the tallest aerial tram in the country, over 4000 feet from valley floor to summit, as the center piece of the new "Jackson Hole Ski Resort." A closer look disclosed runs being cleared of timber off to the right of the towers and several buildings under construction beneath the lowest, at the valley floor. The plan apparently called for a cluster of hotels and services at the base of the tram to be called "Teton Village." Hang on! For the first time since leaving Asheville, my thoughts suddenly returned to the job prospects for a new architect. Where there were buildings being built, there were drawings, and whoever was drawing them might need help. I hadn't even gotten to Jackson yet, but I knew exactly who to look up first once I got settled.

CHAPTER 3

JACKSON, WYO. 1967

C ontinuing on, the East Gros Ventre Butte suddenly cut off the view west and the vast wetland of the Jackson Hole Elk Refuge instead filled my driver's-side window. As I was to learn, winter finds a herd numbering in the thousands there, fed hay in those days from sleds drawn by draft horses plowing through knee-deep snow. The cows and calves clustered in large bands well off the highway, but the bulls gathered by the hundreds alongside the road as if to show off their spectacular racks of antlers to the passing travelers, many of whom pulled over to snap their pictures. Little Mud was oblivious, but I finally got my first glimpse of Jackson, our new hometown, a tiny cluster of humble buildings scattered at the foot of Snow King Mountain. What follows is a description of the place as I first saw it over fifty years ago. Some parts I recall better than others, but if you've been there lately, say since we traded Obama for Trump, you'll get the idea that things there have changed. A lot.

Arriving as I did from the north, the first things you saw were ski runs and a single chairlift aligned vertically with the highway rising up the timbered slopes behind town. At night, lights on the ski-lift made it look from that angle like there was an 1800-foot tall tower standing in front of what the locals called the "Town Hill." It's still in use today but was then a deceptively modest precursor of the grandiose project I'd just seen well underway across the valley; "deceptively," because beginners quickly discovered that there was no easy way down Snow King Mountain. One other thing I remember well about that first taste of Jackson was being slowed to a stop by road construction just short of town. Excited to keep moving, my annoyance with the minor delay was rewarded when we were waved on by an eye-popping twenty-something flag-girl in an electric-red bikini! Whoa! What kind of town is this? A fun town, it turned out, and it still is.

The center of Jackson was and still is marked by the block-long, park-like Town Square. All four of its corners were entered beneath huge pedestrian arches made from thousands of elk antlers woven tightly together, courtesy of the aforementioned vainglorious bulls that shed them out on the Refuge each spring. The north highway had become 'Cache Drive' along the Square's west side and across the street was the still popular "Million Dollar" Cowboy Bar. Gambling had only recently been outlawed in Wyoming, but rumor had it that action could still be found at the Cowboy.

Snow King and the Cowboy Bar, Jackson, Wyo., ca. 1967 -
Photo Unknown

Western bands kept the dance floor full every night and all the bar stools were old beat up saddles that had earned a rest after years riding the range. Street-side, the building sported a brightly colored neon bucking bronco against a weathered board & batten false-front above a shed-roofed wooden boardwalk, just like in the western movies, except real. The other businesses around the Square more or less followed suit.

Between the Cowboy and the corner of Cache and Broadway, the only other paved street in town, Jackson Sporting Goods tended to the needs of tourists, hikers, hunters, fishermen and skiers, each in their seasons. I had no clue at the time, but John Morgan, the building's owner, was to become my employer, partner, life-long friend and major influence in my future life. Continuing around the corner west on Broadway, John's building also housed Virginia's tiny Valley Bookstore and the booking office of Barker-Ewing Float Trips, a summer-only tourist concession in Grand Teton Park. Next, loomed the two-story Wort Hotel, the most impressive building in town.

Wort Hotel, Jackson, Wyo., back in the day. - Photo Unknown

Inside was another happening watering hole in a town with quite a few. The long, curved bar-top was decorated with hundreds of silver dollars embedded in a well-worn epoxy topping. The Wort's Manager, Steve Bartek and his attractive but no-nonsense assistant, Wilma, kept the whole place running and under control. The dining room was the second classiest restaurant in town and always full. Together with the bar and the rooms upstairs, it was favored by the governor, assorted Wyoming politicians and other big-wigs, invariably sporting new-looking cowboy hats, while the summer tourists filled the motels elsewhere and the locals kept to the bar. Wintertime found the latter lined up outside the Wort for the "cutter" races, with two-horse chariots on skids instead of wheels racing down snow-covered Broadway to the cheers of the crowd. Bets were known to have been placed and lots of money often changed hands.

Winter chariot races on Broadway past the Wort Hotel - Photo Unknown

Thinking back, one especially memorable night at the Wort comes to mind. A large meeting room off the bar was the closest thing in town to a convention center. Used for luncheons by Rotary and other business and civic outfits, it could also be set up with a stage, chairs and tables as an occasional Dinner Club. Especially in winter when the few locals needed something to cure their cabin fever, out-of-town talent would be brought in now and then for a show. Everyone in the county turned out. It was a great time to let loose after being holed up for weeks under giant snowdrifts. On one such occasion, a guy billed as an Elvis impersonator was advertised as the entertainment. We all thought we were in for a night of drinking, hooting, hollering and laughter. And we were!

Out he comes, looking slightly pudgy with floppy black hair in an outlandishly ornate Elvis suit, jumping around and pounding out Hound Dog on his guitar. The guy was fabulous. The crowd went wild, pushing tables out of the way to make a dance floor. On and on he went until he'd done every Elvis classic he knew, before taking his first break. What a night! The cocktail waitresses couldn't keep up. There was no back-up act, so a record-player someplace got turned on for awhile. Then, out came a tall, strikingly attractive lady with flaming red hair to announce a change of pace. The next set was to be a medley of popular operas. Operas! They had to be kidding, but they weren't. Elvis now appeared in white tie and tails and the redhead retreated to a chair and picked up a guitar. Together, they put on a show to be remembered. Elvis turned out to be a superb baritone and his lovely accompanist somehow managed to turn her instrument into full-on symphony orchestra. Aida, Rigoletto, The Pirates of Penzance, together, they did them all. It was magical. After each number, the room full of what could only be described as folks 'mixed' in their musical tastes, started giving them standing ovations, hollering "bravo!" and stamping their feet, throwing tens and twenties onto the stage.

Billy Hansen's Exxon was across West Broadway from the Wort. The only gas station right in town, it was pretty much the end of the west side 'business district' except for Roy Jensen's R-J Bar, yet another watering hole three or four blocks further west. The construction crowd favored the RJ, and the cigarette smoke was so thick I thought Roy had it bottled under pressure somewhere in the back and filled the place each day when he opened up. Back at the Square, East Broadway, running the other way from Cache, was home to the Ranch Shop, selling cowboy boots and ten-gallon hats to the hordes of summer tourists, fresh down from feeding the bears in Yellowstone. I did a remodel project for Abi Garaman, the owner, at some point that involved finishing out the huge basement under the retail area as a storeroom. I asked him what they could possibly need so much empty space for, and he replied, "How many pairs of boots do you think we sell every summer?" I had no clue. "A quarter of a million," he answered, and that was back in the 70s! If you're beginning to suspect that there was some money in that little town, even then, you're right. Next door to the Ranch Shop, continuing east was Blake Van de Water's hardware store. You could buy nails by ones or twos and hay from a shed out back.

Blake had figured prominently in one of Paul Petzoldt's more notorious episodes. He was a Forest Ranger at the time, when in a snowy November of 1950, a DC 3 filled with missionaries headed for South America crashed high on the northeast ridge of Mount Moran, a major Teton Peak that dominates the north end of the range. Paul, as the valley's only professional climber at the time, was tasked with leading a team up to the wreckage to see if anyone had survived. He and Blake and two others set out up the ridge to find out. Reaching the crash-site in near-winter conditions, it was clear that everyone aboard was not only killed, but their bodies were crushed inside the twisted remains of the plane and recovery of the victims would be impossible. Returning to the valley, they reported as much to the authorities, the Park Service closed the site to climbers indefinitely, and the matter was forgotten. Well, not entirely. Rumors spread that the plane's occupants had with them a bundle of money with which to start their new enterprise, $50,000 dollars, some said. Where was it? In the wreck? Had the search party found it and kept quiet? They all denied finding sign of any money, but Petzoldt bought a sheep ranch sometime thereafter, and was suspected in some quarters ever after. Blake never talked about the affair at all and having been to the crash site myself several times, I'd be surprised if they found anything at all from inside the plane. It hit a cave-like crevice in the ridge-top and everything had pancaked deeply into the rocks.

Mount Moran, Tetons, NE Ridge right skyline - Photo
Unknown

Next door to Blake's store, the Rancher Bar offered an alternative
to the Cowboy and the Wort for drinkers around the Square looking
for variety. From there to the corner with Center Street were some
rubber tomahawk shops I can't recall, but just beyond, and separated
from the shops by a tiny vacant lot, was the Crabtree Hotel marking
pretty much the east end of what there then was of Jackson's "business
district." The two-story hotel's corner boardwalk and entrance led
into an historic, old-time lodging house with a shared bath down the
hall and appeal to a certain, limited clientele. Tucked in behind the
hotel and fronting onto a continuation of the boardwalk into the
vacant lot was a small, attached outbuilding, home to a pair of businesses that were to figure prominently in my new life. Adjacent to the
hotel, John Horn's Teton Mountaineering was the only source of technical climbing equipment between Denver and Salt Lake City in those
days, and next door, Bob Corbett, licensed member of the American
Institute of Architects (AIA), was overseeing the design of the new ski
resort at Teton Village. Working on several hotels there to house the
newly expected skiers, Corbett, I hoped, would be my meal ticket for
the coming winter and beyond.

Moving on around the Square onto Center Street, Tommy
Benson's Mercantile sat across-corner from the Crabtree and offered

a little bit of everything, like a rough-hewn, proto five & dime store. Upstairs in back, a small toy collection reminded me that my twins, too, were starting their new lives in Jackson Hole and I hoped Tommy had at least two identical versions of every item. Next door, Jim Van Nostrand ran Wyoming Outfitters, a clothing and gear store for the valley's many actual cowboys and cowgirls as well as other locals equally at home on skis in winter and horseback in summer. One or two other shops completed that side of the Square, but just beyond the corner, still on the same side of Center Street was another valley institution, the Jackson State Bank. Presided over by the founder's son, Felix Buchenroth, it was the premier, actually only, financial institution then in town and oversaw the fortunes of cow pokes and high rolling ranchers alike. One of my first projects a year or so later, when I was designing on my own, was a Frank Lloyd Wright look-alike house in town for one of Felix's Loan Officers. The job went well, and he was happy with his fancy, for Jackson, modern new home and spread the word around town that Lee was okay. Felix apparently agreed, because for a long time thereafter, any time I came up short and needed a quick loan, either he or my client would just cut me a check, no questions asked! Those were the days ...

Early D/A 'modern' Jackson residence - Image Vincent R. Lee

Across Center from the bank was Fred's Market, the only grocery store in town. It was set back of a small parking area cut from the corner with Deloney Avenue, bordering the fourth, north side of the Square. A meeting place as well as a food store, Fred's was where you ran into everybody, sooner or later, and found out what was really going on around town. Food occasionally got a bit short in winter, when a big dump came, and avalanches closed all three roads to the outside world. Even still, Fred's always seemed to come through somehow. On down Deloney, Jackson Drug anchored the corner with Cache, where we began our tour. It half-filled the ground floor of a big, two story stone building, other than the Wort the only masonry structure in town that I can recall at that time. I never figured out what was on the second floor, above the drug store, but around the corner on Cache, the other half of the building turned out to be the Teton Theater, showing movies in an old-fashioned auditorium with a curtained stage and big high ceiling.

Elsewhere in town were the County Courthouse, Saint John's hospital, the Elks Lodge, several churches, two lumber yards, a bunch of basic motels and an old two-room, log County Library.

Old log Teton County Library, Jackson - Photo Unknown

Designing a log addition to the latter was another of my early projects, followed by log additions #2, #3, and #4, after which, sometime in the 90s, they moved into a new, modern facility done by an out-of-town firm. At first, having grown up in and among faux suburban "colonials", I had no idea how log cabins were done and relied on local old-time builders to teach me the trade. My modernist professors at Princeton would have pulled my degree if they'd known, but I found it fascinating and the more I learned, the more I liked it. Log-work used a familiar natural material in a totally honest way. What you saw was what you got; nothing hidden, nothing faked, nothing faux. The logs resisting the massive snow loads on the roof were right there above your head, not hidden away in some closed-off attic as though unimportant. Notched tree trunks only gave way to native stone in the foundations and chimneys, where it made sense, not stuck on like wallpaper around the front door to impress visitors. As with the town itself, the leaky old cabins all around town surely had their downsides, but at least they were real.

Maybe "real" is the word that best describes the Jackson Hole I saw the tail end of way back then. Aside from a two-month, Fourth of July-to-Labor Day, tourist season when all hands were on deck dealing with visitors headed to or from Yellowstone, Jackson was pretty much an isolated little cow town surrounded by cattle ranches trying to stay afloat feeding cows over a six-month winter with a single cut of hay put up each season just before snow began to fly in September. Off-season, as the other ten months of the year were called, very few residents had more money than it took to get by. There were successful business people and several wealthy families with large holdings, but few of them wintered over. Those that did were mostly old-time families born and raised in the valley making their livings looking after each other's needs, plus a small colony of eastern refugees that had gone to school and seen the larger world, but preferred the mountains. I guess that was me.

My first spin around the Square, now more than a half century ago, left an impression so strong that I just wrote about it pretty much from memory. If I've gotten anything wrong, chalk it up to more than 80 years of memory use. One thing I'm dead sure of: Jackson wasn't all that pretty in those days, with its billboards, unpaved streets, hodge-podge of mostly beat up old buildings, tourist traps and ugly overhead power lines carelessly strung all over the place, but it was about what I'd expected, and I liked what I saw. Years growing up in the wealthy suburbs of New York had been tempered by four years in the local blue-collar High School. Then, six more in the rarified halls of Princeton were offset by a four-year tour with the Marine Corps and a year working in the Jim Crow South. All of the above had set me on a path to start over, to make my way in a completely new, unfamiliar and wide-open world, and it felt a lot like I'd found that world at last.

CHAPTER 4
SETTLING IN

My first stop in Jackson Hole was the top of the Grand Teton. My pal Ben was also in town as promised, but only had time for one climb before he continued west. Despite Exum's three-year-old offer of a free guided ascent, we opted instead to go for it on our own. After our summer in the Winds, we figured we were up to it and even picked a lesser done, more difficult climb than the standard Upper Exum Ridge favored by the guided parties. The Petzoldt Ridge, paralleling the Exum on the east, struck us as a better challenge, involving both difficult rock and steep snow, much like the climbs we'd been doing with NOLS.

The author on Grand Teton's Petzoldt Ridge, in South Couloir -
Photo Vincent R. Lee

THE ROCK STARTS RIGHT at the level of the usual bivouac site on the Lower Saddle between the Grand and the Middle Teton to the south. About a thousand feet up, the rock climbing ends at the bottom of the South Couloir, a long, steep snow-filled gulley paralleling the easier tourist route to the west and leading straight up to the summit. It was a cold blustery autumn day and we had the mountain pretty much to ourselves. A classic mixed route, it was the perfect kick start for my new life beneath the Tetons.

Ben headed out the next day and I got serious about a job and place to live. Both turned up with surprising ease. I checked in with Corbett first to find out if there was going to be a way to pay the rent. There was. The pace of hotel building at Teton Village was picking up and it was more than he and his lone draftsman, Cliff Poindexter, could handle. I showed them the plans of my North Carolina project, hoping the fairly complicated drawings suggested I knew what I was doing. Bob, of course, and even Cliff were way more experienced than me, but it worked. I was hired on the spot and better yet, told who to talk to about a rental for the coming winter. The contact person escapes me, but whoever it was knew of a small log cabin on one of the big ranches south of town, available until summer when the wealthy owners returned from Arizona. Whoopee! A log cabin on a real ranch out in the wild west! It was exactly what I'd dreamed of. A call to the Owner's local rep confirmed that it was not only still available but would be rent free, and I could move in any time I wanted. Whoa! I was liking Jackson Hole better and better.

Our first "Home on the Range," Melody Ranch, South Park -
Photo Vincent R. Lee

A quick call to New York got Dani and the kids on a plane west
while I started work at Corbett's and unloaded our stuff in the cabin.
It was about five miles out of town on a big cattle outfit called Melody
Ranch. Sure enough, the brand was two linked musical notes. The
polo-playing owner had inherited the ranch from his father, by all
accounts a tough land baron of the old school. His foreman, an
honest-to-goodness cowboy from one of the valley's old families,
greeted me at the ranch entrance. He, too, looked like a tough, no-
nonsense customer, one of many I was soon to meet. The cabin, out
behind the barn, was small, as advertised, with a 'front room,' bath,
kitchen and single bedroom. It looked appropriately rustic, with a
low-pitched metal roof, 3 or 4 small windows, what seemed tight
quarter-pole chinking between the logs and a small covered porch at
the only door. It looked less like the log cabins inevitably shown on
sappy Christmas cards than a set piece from a Clint Eastwood
spaghetti western.

Moving in, I found a couple of features not at first apparent. A line
of ill-fitted fieldstones under the lowest logs appeared to be the 'foundation' and the wood plank floor inside was neither level nor, as far as
I could tell, insulated. Insulation also seemed absent between the wall
logs behind the actually not-so-tight chinking. My new home was

obviously intended as a summer-only place offered to me rent-free so there'd be somebody around the ranch during the months when both the owners and their foreman wisely retired to their winter quarters. Inside, a couple of other design quirks were apparent. The front room was little more than an oversized corridor, with windows and doors to the outside and all three other rooms laid out such that there was hardly any wall space against which to place anything other than a picture or two. It saved on furniture, since all we ended up with was a table and four chairs out in the middle of the room. Finally, the bedroom, intended for a single twin bed, instead barely accommodated two cribs and a double. I don't recall if there was a closet, but there was no room for a dresser. Home sweet home.

Old Jackson Hole airport

Dani and the twins, Scott & Rick - Photo Vincent R. Lee

Dani and the kids arrived the next day on the only flight into town, Frontier's twin turboprop Convair 580 from Denver, scheduled, in those days, several times a week. The tiny airport was just inside the south boundary of Teton Park. The generally favored northern runway approach passes over the park headquarters and visitor center, a detail that continues to plague the uneasy Jackson-Fed relationship to this day. Together again after almost three months apart, ours was a tearful reunion, as you might imagine. I introduced little Mud to them all and it was love at first sight. The twins seemed to have grown a foot since I'd last seen them only three months earlier. Homeward bound, I took them on about the same tour of Jackson that you just read about and I think it fair to say Dani picked up on the downsides quickly, causing me some hesitation to rush her on down to our new "little house on the prairie." Tired from her travels with the two little fellows, though, all she wanted was to get some rest, and off we went. It turned out okay. Finally, after seven years of marriage, we could settle into a home, if not yet a house, of our own.

Work with Corbett, meanwhile, went on without even a day's delay. He was a serious professional and talented designer, but a bit humorless and a workaholic. My fellow employee, Cliff, was another matter. Thank God for him! A farm boy down from the plains of Montana, he'd never studied architecture, but was a born draftsman, artist and flamboyant designer. He'd never been taught all the things an architect isn't supposed to do, as I had, and gave them all a try, did them well and got away with it every time. For me, with my fancy Princeton pedigree, it was sometimes maddening, but he had a hokey western manner about him that people loved, and I did too. We got on immediately and soon formed a silent cabal behind our stern employer's back. Still, office policy included a five and a half-day work week, mandatory half-hour coffee breaks at 10 and 3, always with the boss, and a free hour sharp for lunch. That left Saturday afternoon and Sunday for the rest of your life. That part of my new job was rough, quite the opposite of my year in Asheville, where I was running the project, assisted by an office manager who could have stepped from the pages of a Playboy magazine. The big challenge back there had been keeping your mind and eyes on the work, but I digress.

Office projects with Bob were interesting, varied and I was learning a lot. He left us alone as long as we did our work up to his demanding standards. It reminded me of the Marines, where there wasn't much TLC. They gave you a mission and it was your job to figure out how to get it done - and there was hell to pay if you didn't, so you did. I tended to go to Cliff with questions and he was a fountain of stuff they hadn't taught me at Princeton. Like me, he loved the work of Frank Lloyd Wright and had just moved into an interesting house of his own design, across the valley near the west bank of the Snake River. Our families got together there often. One such snowy Saturday, Cliff and I had put away several beers and came up with the bright idea, late in the afternoon, to ski from his place the five or so miles downstream to our Melody Ranch cabin, east of the river. Once outside, we sobered quickly and focused on the obstacles to be negotiated along the way. At the top of the list was the nearby Snake River, 50 yards wide and only partially frozen. How exactly we got across, I don't recall, but we did and skied on for several hours down South Park, the lower end of the valley, over fields broken only by a single snow-covered road and the occasional top strands of three-wire fences. Not a single building punctuated our route. That was Jackson Hole in the 60s.

Writing about winter brings me back to our little cabin and our family's initiation there. By October, Dani had turned it into a cozy home and she and the boys had come to like it there. Mud, too, had found a happy home, but coyotes were everywhere, howling each night as they pounced on an unlucky rabbit or two. Not yet big enough to stand off one of their hunting packs, we kept the little rascal close after dark. By Halloween it was cold, dark and snowy. By Thanksgiving it was full-on winter. By Christmas, it was 40 below and holding. We'd never seen anything like it. The pipes under the ice-cold floor froze solid and wind would drive snow right through the walls into the rooms wherever the chinking was loose, soon outclassing the gas heater. The drive out to the road was almost always drifted in unless the foreman showed up and bulldozed it open, which was only every now and then. In time, we nevertheless got used to it, having no choice. We were young and it was part of the challenge of getting started in life. Dani was, let's say, stoic, but the kids and Mud loved it, of course, and I secretly did too. What's the point of living in the 'wilderness' unless there's some serious adversity to be overcome?

As the winter wore on and on - and on, however, even my 'mountain man's' taste for adventure began to sour. From my climbing experiences I had come up with my own definition of adventure: anything more fun to anticipate and recall than it was to actually do. Our first Jackson Hole April was proving me right. Work had settled into a routine that got me wondering if I really wanted a career in architecture after all, stuck in an office for the rest of my life, looking out the window. When would I ever get back into the high country? At this rate, never, I thought. Easter came and we didn't even color the kids' eggs. Hidden in the white world outside, they'd not be much fun to look for and be too easy to find. Finally, "mud season" arrived and I could hardly wait to set foot on bare ground. Summer, I knew, wouldn't arrive until June, but even frozen mud would be better than the damned snow. It was classic cabin fever and the wisdom of the locals' 'two-year' rule became vividly apparent. With good reason, Dani, I knew, was wondering what the hell she'd been thinking when she married me. We were both starting to wonder if Jackson Hole was The Place after all.

Jim"Pop"Hollandsworth - Photo Vincent R. Lee

Then, sometime in early May, I got a phone call that not only solved the problem but changed our lives forever. Jim "Pop" Hollandsworth was on the line from Asheville. He had been chosen by the board of the startup Outward Bound school there to be its founding Director. Pop and I had gotten acquainted during my year planning their buildings and discovered we had lots in common. He'd been running an outdoor program at the prestigious Asheville School for Boys for years and believed strongly in the benefits of adventure for young people. His first year with NCOBS had not gone well though, and he was back at Asheville School, planning to incorporate Outward Bound type experiences into his work there. Remembering that I had decamped for Wyoming when the year-round concept had cratered, he'd had an idea: "If I bring a bunch of students out there this summer," he said, "Could you teach them to climb and guide us all up one of the big Teton peaks?" Could I? Are you kidding? I thought. Without the slightest hesitation, I said, "Sure! When are you coming!"

Not thinking it would be a big deal, I mentioned it to Bob the next day at work, adding that it would only be for two weeks and not until July. Oh, and of course I'd take the time off without pay. "Vince, he said. "It looks to me like you're going to have to decide whether you want to be an architect or a mountain climber." True enough, but I figured it was just a rhetorical comment and replied with a grin, "I guess for those two weeks I want to be a mountain climber." "I'll cut you a check this afternoon then," he said with a smile of his own. Yikes! Fired not even a year into my second job! And by the only guy for miles around who could verify my 3-year apprenticeship require-ment with the State Board over in Cheyenne. Dani, I knew, was not going to be happy, especially since Pop had made no mention of paying me for the two weeks. She would correctly put two and two together and get zero. I guess I wasn't a razor-sharp businessman in those days, but not to worry, I thought I might have a fallback plan!

John Morgan, the fellow who owned the Jackson Sporting Goods building on the Square, had been drawing plans for years according to Cliff. He was technically an unlicensed 'designer,' not a registered architect, but his long-time associate, Bob Koedt, an expat Dane I came to like a lot, had just left him to go out on his own. Morgan was thus short a draftsman and might be looking for a replacement. It wouldn't solve the apprenticeship problem, but it might pay the bills. John's office was in the basement of his home, across the valley near the funky little village of Wilson. I gave him a call, downplayed my situation so as not to appear desperate, and found that Cliff was right. John was indeed looking for someone and said to come on over. I had to ask around in Wilson to find his place, up a long rocky drive to a comfortable-looking house partway up the mountainside below Teton Pass. Unlike Corbett, with his office just off the Jackson Square, Morgan was clearly not encouraging walk-in business. His lower level office, drafting room really, since there was no hint of any other activity, was a bit of a mess, made worse by a heavy pall of tobacco. John was a long-time smoker, it turned out, and I wondered if maybe that was one reason Koedt might have left.

The fallback plan wasn't looking all that good after all. When I was a kid, my mother was a smoker. I hated the smell and had never started myself. So, it is a testimonial to John Morgan that we not only hit it off immediately and became fast friends but, in time, business partners as well. For one thing, he was a former Marine, and thus a Semper Fi 'brother,' no matter what, but it also happened he was just then quitting cigarettes. Not only that, but he'd decided to move the office out of his basement and into an upstairs space in one of the buildings on Skyline Ranch, a 600-acre spread between Jackson and the Snake River he'd just bought in partnership with two other friends. Thus was born Design Associates, with John as the principal and me as the founding associate. My new boss upped my pay from Corbett's a bit and, better yet, said I could go climbing anytime I wanted, which I did. A potential disaster had miraculously morphed into a win-win-win! This unexpected turn of events allowed me to spin the whole thing as promotion of sorts with Dani, who also thought it meant I'd be home more. I hoped she was right, and it seemed I had clearly dodged a domestic bullet for the time being.

John Morgan - Photo Morgan Family

The only downside to the switch was that Cliff and I drifted apart once I left Corbett's. He and I had secretly tossed around the idea that both of us might one day quit and open our own shop. Teton Village was beginning to catch on, and not only more new hotels, but ski lodges and private homes were starting to pour into Corbett's office, more than he could handle. Cliff and I had figured we could pick up the slack and make a go of it. In time, he did open his own shop with another talented designer and the two of them did well, eventually becoming prime competitors of Design Associates. They were so successful they even bought the Cowboy Bar as a sideline. The town of Jackson, having historically lived on cattle, dude ranching and a two-month-long summer Yellowstone tourist season, was starting to develop a new winter prosperity unheard of only a few years earlier. The entire valley was awakening to the prospect of a brand new booming year-round future, and almost everyone including me thought it was terrific! Those rust-proof-orange tram towers I'd spotted coming into town that first day were destined to be worth more money than if they'd been the steel head frames of fabulous new gold mines.

Original Teton Village clock tower and Base Station - Photo Unknown

CHAPTER 5
GOLDEN EGGS

B efore I launch at last into my role as a "small town architect" in the transformative drama about to unfold, you should know that Pop Hollandsworth did indeed arrive with a van load of teen aged Asheville School boys that July. I taught them climbing in the Tetons and we spent two weeks in the Winds, finally summiting Gannett Peak, Wyoming's highest at 13,804 feet.

Asheville School group en-route to Gannett Peak, left, 1968 - Photo Vincent R. Lee

Pop and his friend "Doc" Lindsley helped out and a good time was had by all. The trip became the first of several epic adventures with Pop and his students. Not only did I get paid well for the trips, the program eventually morphed into a full-on mountaineering school named High Country West, Alpine Adventures, initially co-directed by Pop and me. A single three-week program each summer soon became two, and then three sessions, a week apart in June, July and August. By the early 70s, Asheville had wisely divested itself of the program, and though Pop continued to participate until his retirement several years later, I found myself running the whole show. Miraculously, HCW's growing list of former students all lived to tell the tale and most, I like to think, went home from the experience better than when they arrived. The story is told in full in another of my books, Old School, A Mountain Guide's Life Before the Net. The answer to Corbett's question had revealed itself: it looked like I'd be a mountain climber and an architect. The whole episode fits into the tale told here largely as it impacts Dani's expectation, noted earlier, that I'd be "home more." Uh oh...

John and I got right to work setting up shop in the new space at Skyline Ranch so we could begin harvesting the "golden eggs" that the "goose" of Jackson Hole was about to lay. It was 1968 and the idea that D/A, as we called our fledgling practice, might somehow contribute to endangering that goose was nowhere on the radar. Aside from Jackson, Wilson and "The Village," as the new ski area was being called, there were about 75,000 acres of privately-owned sagebrush, woods and hayfields in the valley. What difference would a few new houses here and there make? We quickly discovered that neither John nor I had time to design, draw and oversee our projects and run a business. This was long before computer assisted drafting (CAD) and we were spending hours putting pencil to paper on our drafting tables. We hired a secretary/office manager, Susan Shaver, to take care of everything else and with her help slicked up the office a bit to show a better face to prospective clients. We chose a rust-colored shag carpet - it was the 70s after all - to lighten things up. The only down-side to the space was the fly problem. It was an old building and they came in from every crevice. Try as we did to stop them it never worked. We vacuumed them live off the windows and dead from the floor every morning before opening for work and came to think of the official D/A office colors as "shag carpet orange and housefly black."

My very first architectural client turned out to be me. Our cabin in South Park was only available until the ranch owners returned from Arizona in late July. John urged me to take advantage of the VA loan benefit from my time in the Marines and build a house of my own. Until then, I had no idea such a benefit even existed, but I applied, was approved for a loan of $17,500 and began looking for land. A new real estate office had sprouted in town run by Art Brown and Orrin Soest. Transplanted easterners like me, they were among the first of what was to become a veritable host of others casting hungry eyes on the above mentioned 75 K of theoretically salable, eminently buildable acres of open land. For me, they found a five-acre parcel at the end of Wenzel Lane, a dead-end dirt road south off Wyo. 22 on the Wilson side of the Snake River that would one day come to be called the "West Bank." The only other people out there at the time were By Kellam, another aspiring realtor, and a plumber from New Jersey named Jack Graham. Each had his own five acres to the east of those Brown was offering to me.

He wanted twenty grand, a mind-boggling amount of money at the time, more than my entire loan, so I kept on looking. Not to lose a sale, Art came back with new offer. He said he'd split the property into four one and a quarter-acre parcels and sell me one for five thousand bucks, and that was the best he could do. That left me $12,500 for the minimum three-bedroom house required by the VA rules. The building site was a formerly irrigated hayfield with uninterrupted south sun and great western and northern view of the Tetons. The design I came up with, intended to compliment the stark horizontality of the land, was a single-story, slab-on-grade, broad flat-roofed rectangle of concrete blocks. It was open to the south but insulated elsewhere by earth berms pushed into place with an old bulldozer John used to keep his driveway open in winter. Our new house was basic shelter, as it had to be, and not much of a crowd-pleaser. The word quickly got around that the new people out on Wenzel Lane were some sort of Eastern aliens, living in a square flying saucer, stranded out in the tall grass. The $12.5 K from the VA hadn't quite been enough, and I borrowed another thousand from my dad, but for $18,500 we had a cozy little house and our own home and land in Jackson Hole within a year of our arrival. One of the things I recall most fondly about that little place is how quiet it was. Even in the daytime, we could hear the Snake River, half a mile away. Today, it seems, pretty much all one hears, anywhere in the valley, is traffic.

Wenzel Lane house, winter of 1969 - Photo Vincent R. Lee

I thought it a great design and still do, but being my first actually built, it had its flaws. Tom Lamb, the VA inspector and owner of one of the two lumber yards in town, said he had his doubts about a flat roof in snow country. He was worried about the loads, but I convinced him I'd planned for that and it turned out the wind actually kept it pretty clear in winter anyway. Snowmelt or rain were the problems. As any builder knows, there's really no such thing as a 'flat' roof, and water ponded here and there, soon leaking between the layers of tar paper constituting the old fashioned 'built-up' roof. Also unwelcome inside were close relatives of the houseflies over at the office. They came in everywhere, congregating on the warm, south-facing windows. Tom thought the screening of the roof vents might be the problem, so I went around the eaves spraying DDT, or whatever it was, into the openings, thinking to discourage flies from coming in. Quite a few crazed flies immediately tumbled out and spiraled satisfyingly to their deaths, hinting that Tom had been right. Thinking problem solved, I turned to head inside only to hear a scream and be met by Dani bolting out the door in panic. Pressing on, I found the floor, furniture and everything else completely covered with what seemed millions of flies, buzzing in their death throes, being joined by millions more fleeing every crack into the interior. It was a scene from an Alfred Hitchcock horror movie. Dani refused to even go near the house until I'd filled untold numbers of vacuum bags with the doomed, buzzing critters, but as at D/A, we never truly got rid of them.

It was about that time, 1969, that another somewhat more ambitious design failure gave everyone in the valley a good laugh. The Teton Pass road had long been plagued by winter avalanches. Most were west of the crest, but 10,086-foot Mt. Glory, looming above Wilson produced the most reliable. It ran several times a season, closing traffic for days and was a bit scary between slides. Someone had even been killed years earlier. Wyoming's Department of Transportation, WDOT, had finally decided enough was enough. Time to solve the problem once and for all. Pointy-heads over in Cheyenne decided that the solution was an avalanche bridge, to be the nation's first, over the slide path as part of a massive realignment of the entire highway. The Mt. Glory Slide had denuded a huge hour-glass-shaped swath of the steep eastern mountainside and the new right-of-way crossed exactly at the midpoint. All the snow from the upper 'accumulation zone' passed through this 'narrows' on its way to the 'deposition zone' at the bottom. The bridge was to span the slot between the two, theoretically an elegant solution. Knowledgeable locals told them it was crazy and favored instead a 'snowshed' over the exposed roadway, as other mountain areas with the same problem had been building for years.

Season one of the three allotted to the project found the new roadbed roughed in, interrupted by a two-hundred-foot gap between two huge concrete abutments. From their brinks it was seventy feet straight down to the narrow gulley's floor but measured normal to the slope it was only about thirty. A large crane left standing on the near side of the chasm was knocked off by the very first slide that winter and found in twisted ruins at the bottom of the hourglass once the snow melted in July. Hmm, this tip-off that the scheme was flawed went unheeded in Cheyenne. Season two found the road nearly done and two monstrous steel catenary arches spanning the gap with the steel framework for the deck remaining to be completed in season three. I skied up there at some point in late February and discovered that the arches, while parallel, had been bent slightly downhill! Studies done belatedly after the fact found that the snow passing through the narrows was sometimes as much as eighty feet deep and moving at over a hundred miles per hour! The bridge never had a chance. The arches were taken down and scrapped. The road was bulldozed deeper into the mountainside and filled right across the slide path, directing traffic momentarily into and out of harms way. Army surplus artillery pieces were stationed below and manned by trained Highway Department guys who, to this day, blow the hell out of the Glory Slide many a winter morning to bring down slides before they can build up.

Bent avalanche bridge - Photo Unknown

Post bridge Mt. Glory slide path - Photo Unknown

Meanwhile, real clients soon discovered our little firm and new commissions began coming in from John's long-time valley friends and neighbors as well as people like me, new to Jackson Hole. Among the former was Bill Ashley, part-owner of Jackson Sporting Goods in John's building on the Square. Bill and Mary lived in an old log house in town, right at the base of Snow King Mountain, the Town Hill. It had 'character,'

but no sun. It faced due north and there were still snowbanks around the place when I went there in July to discuss the project with them. The Ashleys had bought a beautiful building lot in the new Skyline Ranch subdivision, a wooded part of the land our office was on. John and his partners had split up about a third of the property in order to pay for the ranch. Bright, sunny, warm and with a "view of the Grand," as the realtors had come to describe the ultimate and most costly Jackson Hole amenity, the Ashleys' site had only a single draw-back. It overlooked an irrigated hayfield and the mosquitos all through June and July were so horrendous, we always conducted our frequent site visits together sitting in a closed car with the A/C running. Bugs be damned, the project nevertheless inspired another of my favorite designs.

A RESIDENCE FOR MR. AND MRS. BILL ASHLEY   D|A

Ashley Residence Rendering - Image Vincent R. Lee

Foolishly thinking they might want a more upscale log home than their place in town, I first proposed one. "Are you kidding? Hell no!" they said, "We've been cooped up in that damned dark, leaky old place for years! We want something modern, with lots of glass and open space." I heard the same over and over again from John's fellow long-time valley residents and soon found that it was only the newcomers that wanted romantic log "cabins." The old timers had grown up living with them and were long overdue for something new and better. As a result, my designs never degenerated into a personal "style." I did both old and new, large and small, always taking what my clients said they wanted and trying to produce it for them as sensibly, economically and artfully as I could. My personal input into the process was to take maximum advantage of the natural amenities and features of their properties, disturbing them as little as possible so that the resulting structures "fit in" both physically and visually to their surroundings.

Thinking that in doing so I was helping to preserve and celebrate Nature, I was in fact adding one more building, with its roads, utilities and need for services to a place where previously none of those things had existed. Before I was through, I'd done it several hundred times and was only one of scores of other architects doing exactly the same thing. Interestingly, none of that occurred to me as problematic at the time. Looking back, I have no regrets about it and am still proud of many, if not most of my creations. The clients typically loved their new homes, and some remained good friends long after their projects were done. A few even came back for seconds and several for thirds. Even early on, some were memorable. Take Robert Goulet, for example. Other movie stars and Hollywood people sometimes vacationed at the valley's several dude ranches, and various "western" productions like Shane and The Mountain Men had been filmed there, but Goulet was the first to buy and build a house. Actually, he wanted a big addition to a small stone cottage John had done years earlier atop the aforementioned East Gros Ventre Butte, overlooking the Elk Refuge. John was tied up on another project and I got the job.

Goulet and his wife Carol Lawrence, another star, were playing at one of the big Vegas casinos. This was before a rather nerdy Wayne Newton reinvented himself into the Strip's iconic "bad boy" of more recent times. To fend off unwanted phone calls from zealous fans, the Goulets both took only calls from those privy to their secret passwords. Mr. Goulet's was "ROGO," and I was admitted to the inner circle for the duration of the project. The hotel operator would say, "How may I help you?" to which I'd respond "ROGO." She'd come back with "Please hold, I'll put you through." The Goulets were very private when in town for site visits and sometimes brought friends and family with them for company. On one such occasion, I arrived to find an elderly woman on her hands and knees scrubbing the flagstone entry floor. Ms. Lawrence and Rogo both greeted me warmly and he called to the woman, "Hey mom, come in and meet our architect."

By and large, the movie crowd seemed to prefer the older ski resorts like Aspen and Sun Valley and later, Jackson's arch-competitor, Telluride. An exception was Harrison Ford. By the time he showed up in the early 80s, I'd begun another life with another wife and a shared side career in Andean archaeology, all to be described in more detail later. Inspired initially by a book I'd read titled Antisuyo, by a flamboyant and vaguely mysterious American explorer named Gene Savoy, I found myself daydreaming about what it would be like to search for "lost cities" in the jungles of Peru, as he had. My time in the Marines had taught me a few lessons about getting along in the tropical forest and I thought I was up to the challenge. I was still mulling over the idea when I first saw Ford's 1981 film, Raiders of the Lost Ark. The early scenes were supposedly set in the depths of the Amazon and had clinched the deal for me. I became so determined to head for the cloud forests of Peru, that my costume for the upcoming, valley-wide Halloween bash had me outfitted as an explorer with a bloody arrow protruding from his back. Clever as I thought it was, the arrow repeatedly poked other dancers and everyone else around me, bringing angry demands that I get the hell off the floor out of their way! I did, but with another interested friend, laid the plans that very night for the first of what would become many exploring expeditions and a new 'career' in archaeology.

As a brief aside, one evening sometime thereafter following our return from just such an adventure, we met the Fords at a fundraising dinner in Jackson and someone mentioned my new Raiders-like Peruvian pastime. Suddenly interested, the star's then wife Melissa Mathiesen, who'd written the script for ET the Extraterrestrial, turned to Ford and said, "Harry, here's a guy who actually does all that Indiana Jones stuff." A bit sheepishly, Ford added, "Actually, we filmed those scenes in Hawaii, but I'd love to go to Peru someday!" Sure enough, as I later confirmed, that mysterious-looking peak behind Raiders' opening credits is indeed not far off the main highway outside Kauai's capital, Lihue. Ford and I became better acquainted several years later, serving together on the Board of the local Land Trust, but I never did any work for him. Those that did told me he was quite a demanding client. Before getting into the movies, he'd apparently been a carpenter and took a very hands-on approach to his Jackson Hole building projects.

CHAPTER 6
"INTERESTING TIMES"

Most of our projects in those early years were not for the rich and famous. Both John and I designed lots of modest homes for valley residents and newcomers alike. Some of my favorite projects weren't homes at all. I was asked to design a new refuge to replace the old Quonset hut on the Lower Saddle between the Grand and Middle Tetons. It had been used for years by Exum's guides and Park personnel needing shelter high on the mountain, but it was in bad shape. My design, housed within two large, heli-lifted steel culverts, clearly met the two criteria: minimal site disturbance and ease of removal if needed but was too high-tech for the times. They instead put up a pair of strong-backed tents. I had more success with my scheme for a covered outdoor cooking shelter at the American Alpine Club's then new Climber's Ranch up in the Park. Done in the 70s, it still stands well-used and is featured in the Club's brochure describing the Ranch facilities.

American Alpine Club cooking shelter, Grand Teton Park -
Photo Vincent R. Lee

Doing a wide variety of projects, we got to know the local builders and sub contractors well. We came to avoid a few but liked most and some became our favorites. I learned construction by paying attention to them and their work. Among my first of such teachers was Jake Bruner. A craggy-good-looking mountaineer and expert skier originally from Switzerland, Jake was an old-school perfectionist and had the 'carriage trade' out at Teton Village locked up tight. His German accent and Alpine charm won over the ladies every time. He worked only cost-plus and got a 15 % fee on top of everything, both unheard of at a time when most projects were competitively bid, and contractors were lucky to get even ten percent. His motto was, "Why use a 2x4 when a 2x6 will do?" The wives got gorgeous second and third homes and their well-heeled husbands paid the large tabs. I liked Jake a lot and he did my very first big fancy house at the Village, for a wealthy couple from back East. Jake and his crew took me under their wings and showed me how to deal with discerning clients and produce the quality results they expected. The job went well, the house was, unlike my own, a definite crowd pleaser and it paved the way for a number of rewarding, similar village projects over the years to come.

Brunner Construction's framing foreman was Ben Mateosky, a big 'builder's-builder' who later founded his own high-end company over in town. All of Jake's finish work was overseen by Les Weber, a mild-

mannered guy who knew more about wood and how to use it prop-
erly than anyone else in the valley. When Les, too, later quit Jake and
started Weber Construction, he and I did lots of interesting jobs
together, many of them using logs. The rest of the Brunner crew was
made up of seasonally out-of-work mountain guides and off-duty ski
patrolmen, many of whom in time also ended up with their own
contracting businesses. By his fine example, Jake unintentionally gave
birth to much of his own competition. Before splitting off, his
younger workers were a fun-loving bunch and let loose after work
each day at the Sojourner Bar in the basement of one of the earliest
Village hotels. Designed by John Morgan with help from Bob Koedt, it
was a powerful, authentically Alpine-looking structure, the best one
out there, I always thought, possibly benefiting from Koedt's
European continental background.

Original Alpenhof Lodge and Sojourner Inn, Teton Village -
Photo Unknown

From the outset, the developers of the Jackson Hole Ski Corporation had decided on a European 'look' for the project not unlike that
favored at most US ski resorts at the time. A few in Colorado super-
imposed Swiss detailing over mining camp Victorian, but the results

always seemed to me fake, foreign and a bit silly. Why not use logs and stone, the home-grown architectural tradition of the Northern Rockies? I thought.

No one picked up on my unspoken idea and the make-believe juggernaut of Disneyesque design continues to this day. Full disclosure: lest you think me a self-righteous prig, however, I ended up doing a beautiful "Swiss" chalet for the owner of another of the earliest Village hotels, the upscale Alpenhof Lodge. Just across the muddy, unpaved parking area from that hotel and the adjacent Sojourner, the late 60s also saw construction of two no-frills early Teton Village favorites. The Hostel provided a lot of badly needed down-scale rooms, but not much else, and next door, the Mangy Moose filled the gap with affordable food and drinks. Planned primarily as a rustic, apres-ski bar, the "Moose" came close to my idea of a genuine Wyoming article. Conceived and built by Denny Becker largely with an all-ski-patrol crew, it followed the dictates of a then popular book. Your Engineered House, by a guy named Rex Roberts. Rex's motto might have been the opposite of Brunner's: "Why use finished lumber when green, rough-sawn boards will do?" Framed with free-standing, unpeeled lodgepole pine posts and built of pine planks straight from Joe Pivik's old sawmill just south of Wilson, it was a no-nonsense, frontier-looking place. Cheap to build, hard to heat and virtually damage-proof, it looked to me and most everyone else like pure old time Jackson Hole.

The unfinished ground floor was intended for future shops. Upstairs, the Moose tavern was a single barn-like space with mezzanine balconies all around under a timber-framed, low-pitched roof. Steel tie-rods spanned across between the posts to resist the Village's monster snow loads. Access to the bar level was via broad timber stairway rising gently from the parking lot straight up to a pair of big, sturdy-looking double entry doors. The Grand Opening arrived on a cold, snowy January night and promised to be an event to remember. Dani and I were on hand, expecting a good party. We were not disappointed. Incongruously, a Doors sound-alike band from over in heavily Mormon Idaho was booked for the event. Remember, this was still the 60s. The place was packed. Everyone was soon drunk and the band was great! Even so, things picked up, literally with a bang, when early in the evening several ski patrolmen and other members of Denny's crew burst through the front doors riding snow machines, having raced up the snow-covered stairway from the parking lot at full speed. A bit later, a memorably well-endowed female celebrant who shall remain un-named demonstrated her approval by swinging across the room topless, hand over hand on one of the steel tie-rods. A cheer went up. The Moose was officially OPEN!

Mangy Moose Saloon, Teton Village - Photo The Mangy Moose

Nights like that were weekly events in those days for some, but not for Dani and me. Things were about to change along the lines of the old Chinese curse: May you live in interesting times. The late 70s were destined to be such times for us both. Our third son, Christopher, had arrived in 1969 and looking after the three boys took up most of Dani's time. Money was always a problem. To help with family finances, she gamely put her considerable artistic talents to work making jewelry for sale to friends, neighbors and tourists. We bought a knitting machine with which she added handsome ski sweaters to her line, briefly sharing shop-space in the finally finished basement of the Moose with several other artisans. Meanwhile, wintertime found me working six and sometimes seven ten-hour days at D/A, turning out the endless drawings needed for our clients' burgeoning projects. CAD was still far in the future and everything was hand-drawn with pencils on tracing paper. There yet being no local print shop, we had to run multiple sets of our own "blueprints" one at a time on our monster old printing machine. Everything took hours.

John had taken me in as a partner in the early 70s, when work had begun pouring in, but he was now becoming tired of the grind. Computerized 'word processing' hadn't yet come along and we bought Sue an IBM 'Selectric' typewriter with which she continued to produce the specs, correspondence and billing plus doing the payroll and books. To that we added interior design services, such that she was doing everything except designing the buildings and drafting the plans. To help with the latter, we started hiring draftsmen. Our first helped us briefly but soon left and started his own firm, still prominent in Jackson as I write this. We had thus begun spawning our own competition, much as Jake Brunner had done earlier. Others also filled in for a few months before moving on to warmer climes or other offices. A fellow climber and student friend from my grad school years at Princeton, Phil Hocker, came west, signed on and became a D/A stalwart for a number of years. Phil and I remain pals to this day.

Another partner, Tom Muths, joined the firm around the same time. A registered Wyoming architect, he enabled D/A to begin doing "public" work not permitted by state law to unlicensed 'designers' like John and me. By putting his stamp on all of our drawings we legally became "Design Associates, Architects." Once he was onboard, our workload expanded into schools, commercial spaces like the Ranch Shop project noted earlier and government jobs including all four Library additions. John had done a small law office some years prior in nearby Pinedale and Tom revitalized that market with several municipal projects there. A personal benefit of my work with him was that his presence counted toward the apprenticeship I needed to be eligible for the state licensing exam in Cheyenne. My time in Asheville and not-quite-a-year at Corbett's office left me with another year remaining due and my year-plus with Tom filled the gap. I promptly took and passed the exams and got my Wyoming license. By the time all that had happened, though, John and I were starting to revisit the decision to expand the firm. With six of us then in the office, he and I found ourselves hustling work all the time in order to keep everyone else busy. Neither of us liked that. Some knotty partnership problems had also been simmering for awhile and they finally came to a head. The details aren't important here, but we finally dissolved the partnership, Tom set up his own practice in Jackson and John retired, leaving what was left of D/A to yours truly.

In theory, it was a great step forward for me, now a self-employed architect with my own firm. The reality was that I was now running D/A while also being sole owner of HCW, a second business that kept me out of the office for the three-month climbing season each summer in a place with at most a six-month fair-weather building season. Juggling both enterprises seemed, at times, more than a full-time job. On top of all that, matters at home were ever more pressing. At age twelve, in 1973, the twins had become interested in the Boy Scouts and we decided to start our own Wilson troop, #40, sponsored by Jay Hess's Stagecoach Bar, below Teton Pass. Soon, all 21 kids west of the river were members with me as their part-time Scoutmaster. Our specialties were mountain climbing and skiing and we became regionally famous for our 1975 ascent of the 13,770-foot Grand Teton.

Wilson's Troop 40, BSA atop the 13,770-foot Grand Teton -
Photo Vincent R. Lee

Other troops began asking that we take them climbing as well, and we did trips all over the northern Rockies. It was great fun, but it too took time away from both work and home. Finally, as will be featured a bit later, my strong, long-standing love of Nature and interest in conservation led me briefly into politics and then more deeply into public service in environ-mental affairs. In short, I was stressed out and next to never home. Whether it was because of the press of all the above responsibilities, or whether all that activity was unconsciously intended to keep me away is a good question. In either case, the effect was the same, and it wasn't good.

Dani and I had been drifting apart for some time, but the compli-cated and time-consuming new circumstances finally broke the back of our eighteen-year marriage, and in 1978, we divorced. As with the earlier breakup of the D/A partnership, the details aren't important, but I could see that there was no future in which both Dani and I could be happy together, and I left her. I'm not proud of how it all unfolded, but I was sure it was the right thing to do and the many subsequent years have proven me right. We didn't fight over children or home. She kept the house on Wenzel Lane and our three boys stayed living there with my support. She soon went on to remarry, however, divorce a second time and marry yet again, I think happily the last time around. Initially, our boys hardly understood what was happening or why. They correctly held me responsible, though, and we began an unsatisfyingly tense, once-a-week relationship that was hard on us all. In time, they drifted back to me more than their new stepfathers and eventually we all adjusted to the new reality pretty well. Some years later, with the boys grown, Dani sold the little Wenzel Lane house for almost 30 times what we'd paid for it in 1968 and moved across the state to Sheridan with her third husband.

For me, the upside of all this trauma was a renewed sense of freedom, as a weight that had held me down for years was lifted. I loved my work, both in the mountains and at the drafting table and pursued both with renewed vigor. Needing a place to live, I briefly moved into the office while renovating the upper level of the old Skyline Ranch granary building next door as a loft apartment. It turned out well and keeping me company moving in was my old dog Mud, now 11 years old and typical of aging large dogs, her hind quarters were starting to fail. I set up a special hooch for her in the new 'mud room'

Granary being remodeled as a home/office for HCW & D/A -
Photo Vincent R. Lee

I'D ADDED to the granary and for awhile, all went well. She was free to come and go at will and hung around our new home faithfully when I was away working at the office, which was a lot. Friends took care of her when I was in the mountains. The arthritis finally became crippling, though, and I think she just slept most of the time. She had trouble getting up and got to where her hind legs hardly worked at all. I should have put her down, but we'd been pals so long, I just couldn't do it. One blustery winter day with new snow piling up, I came home from lunch and she was gone. There were no tracks to follow, nothing to suggest where she'd gone. I looked everywhere, but never found her. Expecting I'd find her bones in the spring, there was never a trace. She'd had the courage to do what I hadn't had the guts to do. Strange as it may sound, given all the turmoil in my life at that time, my treatment of Mud at the end of her life remains possibly my most lasting regret.

Ever since the D/A breakup, the office workload had been tapering off. In '78, we'd booked 18 new projects, but in '79 it was down to 9 and by 1980 there were only 6. Among other reasons, the election of Ronald Reagan in 1980 caused interest rates to plummet, spreading unease in a speculative real estate market based on previously accelerating rates. A number of our clients put their projects on hold or cancelled them altogether. Phil and then Sue soon ran out of work and had to find other jobs. It was a sad time at D/A. But for the sale of a vacant lot next to the Wenzel Lane house that I'd earlier purchased and salvaged from the divorce, I'd have been pretty nearly broke. Finally working now alone and no longer needing the old D/A office space, I moved my practice into a shared, one-room office with my friend Denny Emory, a fellow Princeton architect just then starting out on his own. We joked that we we'd also become ruthless competitors, hard at work shoulder to shoulder in the same tiny garret above the neighborhood food market at "The Aspens," a new up-scale subdivision along the lone road to rapidly expanding Teton Village. We had fun working together there cranking out our respective jobs but adjourning daily to Happy Hour at the lively bar next door, a welcome amenity of our new venue.

As if to put an exclamation point at the end of this otherwise dispiriting period of my life, in 1979, the winter after I moved alone into the remodeled granary and started work in the "studio" office Denny and I were sharing, the valley hit its first major growth bump. Development at the Village, The Aspens and all along "Rabbit Row," as the Village road had been dubbed due to the houses sprouting everywhere alongside the highway, had blossomed to the point that a new power line was needed to carry the increased electrical load. Ever mindful of aesthetic values, WDOT planners in Cheyenne had thoughtlessly followed up their avalanche bridge debacle by permitting the local Power Cooperative to erect a row of large pylons in the scenic margin of Highway 22, the busiest route in the valley, from Jackson to its intersection with Rabbit Row. To this day, this power corridor stands directly between the traveling public and a magnificent panorama of the Teton Range. The picturesque ranch foreground of which has, however, since been forever protected by conservation easement and the WDOT project avenged when seventeen of the offending towers along the final stretch to the Village blew down in a 2017 blizzard.

The new conductor cables, meanwhile, needed to make a hard-right turn north out to the ski area at the corner of 22 and Rabbit Row. To brace the oversized corner tower, guy wires were strung across 22 to a second tower firmly guyed and anchored into massive concrete abutments. The engineers, savvy to the whims of nature, anticipated shrinkage of the conductors and guy wires by designing in enough slack to accommodate winter temperatures of minus fifty, Fahrenheit, a full ten degrees colder than anyone could remember ever happening. Along came December 31st, and the thermometer read sixty-four below zero at my place, less than half a mile from the double towers at the corner. It was reportedly seventy below up in Yellowstone.

Despite the beautifully clear, calm weather, everyone's vehicles were literally frozen in place. Stopped clocks all said about 2AM, confirming that power had gone out all over the valley during the previous night. The cross-corner guy wires had all snapped and, worse, sprung back, wrapping themselves around all the conductors, shorting out the entire system. Wood fires blazed everywhere there was a stove or fireplace, but alas, not in the many empty palaces of absentee owners. Fire-smoke soon dimmed the sun as everyone's pipes froze and broke, even where clever architects like me had kept them well away from outside walls. It was a mess, but the plumbers and contractors had an icy field day, unappreciated at the time, but enjoyed the following summer, lounging in their brand-new boats and RVs. As a footnote, I finally got my vehicle running by dragging it through the snow out to the highway with the ranch tractor, all four wheels frozen, and continued dragging it on the pavement until they broke free. Crossing the bridge over Fish Creek going into Wilson for the mail, I noticed several moose hunched down in the ice-free mid-stream current with nothing but their nostrils, eyes and ears visible. Thinking how cold it must be in the water, it dawned on me that it was actually over 100 degrees warmer there than on the bridge above!

No mail had gotten through, so I returned to the steadily freezing Granary just in time to get a call from my buddy Jim LaRue reminding me that we had agreed to do some ice climbing that weekend up in Montana, north of the Park. Better yet, he said, it was only forty below up there. Not having much to keep me sitting alone by my wood stove, I figured, what the hell? Why not? and off we went. Jim, twenty years my junior and even crazier than me where climbing was concerned, had become a close friend and one of my most reliable guides at HCW. Winter ice routes around Jackson Hole all involved ski approaches, unappealing at sixty below, but we'd heard that there was great ice right above the road north of the Beartooth Mountains near Red Lodge, so that's where we went. Sure enough, the very first place we found was a big frozen waterfall just off the highway. Getting onto the ice, however, called for a couple of hundred feet of scrambling up easy, snow-covered ledges, so up we went, hoods up and mittens on. Arriving at the ice, we began getting the climbing gear out of our packs, each thinking the other had the rope. Neither of us did, but a glance down at my VW solved the mystery. There it was on top of the car, far below. Down climbing those same 'easy' ledges in the snow without a rope was too spooky even for us, and it took us the rest of the day to find a safe way back to the car.

So ended New Year's Eve, 1979. Well, not quite. Once back on the road we headed for the nearest town, Absorkee, a bustling fly-fishing center in summer. Now, it was closed up tight except for the Absorkee Bar, the perfect place, we thought, to make up for our mountaineering fiasco. The place was packed with every local for miles around and live entertainment was being provided by a solo guy playing four or five different instruments simultaneously, a One-Man- Band, and he was good! We had more New Year's fun that night than any I can remember. The locals thought we were nuts, out climbing frozen rocks and icicles in 40 below cold and kept on buying us drinks all night as if we were heroes. Being far from that, it finally dawned on us that we needed a place to stay for the night and we learned that the closest place would be in Red Lodge, 40 miles by the main highway, but only 20 by the 'short cut'. In our condition, the short cut seemed the obvious choice, despite warnings from our new friends that it wasn't plowed. The wind, we found, had nevertheless kept it clear for the first 10 or 12 miles, but then drifts began turning up every few yards. The solution we came up with was to step on it and hit them hard enough to punch on through, and it worked until about five miles out of Red Lodge where one stopped us cold. Once our momentum was lost, so were we until an old rancher with a shotgun and tractor saved us from ourselves at 2AM on January 1st, 1980.

CHAPTER 7
MORE AND BIGGER EGGS

Fortunately, the Chinese curse was not to last. By the early-80s, interest rates had settled down, the real estate market had picked up and the increasingly world-renowned Jackson Hole Ski Resort had caught on big-time creating a vigorous all-season economy. New developments were being stimulated all over Jackson Hole south of Grand Teton Park, but especially west of the Snake. A growing phalanx of realtors quickly latched onto the name "West Bank" there to enhance the prestige appeal and up prices on that side of the valley. It worked. Most of my projects formerly 'on hold' came back to life and new clients began pouring in. The Aspens rapidly built out with both condos and residences, more than a few designed by me. Hayfields were sliced up for subdivisions and the gold rush was back on. Just south of our office, Jackson's first gated community, called "Teton Pines," was looking for the well-heeled to buy pricey lots in the woods surrounding a new short-season golf course, the valley's second. Berms and ponds had been built and new trees planted to enhance land cleared and leveled years earlier by pioneer ranchers. One, Earl Hardeman, with a neighboring cow outfit said of the new development across the fence, "I hope it works. It'll be a hell of a place to hay if it doesn't!"

The fenced Club grounds had two entrances, one protected by a guard station manned by uniformed mall-cops taking turns patrolling in official-looking pickups. The other was exit-only, secured by an electric gate. It all looked very safe and exclusive, though who the bad guys were remained unclear, since 90% of the traffic in and out was construction-related, flooding the inner sanctum each day with scores of plumbers, electricians, carpenters, sheet-rockers, roofers and other tradesmen. Everyone was routinely waved through by the 'cops,' hardly looking up from their little guardhouse. In no time, the 'secret' code for the back gate was well known by almost everyone and since it was closer to town, half the traffic went through that way. The gated feature was just a silly real estate scam designed only to add 'prestige' to an otherwise plain-old high-end subdivision. The lots around the fairways were, however, gorgeous and before long I had designed more homes for them, six, than any office in town. One commanded a spectacular view straight up the driving range. I called for expensive safety glass in the picture windows on that side just in case, and both they and the deck on that side took occasional hits. The Club finally put up a huge net.

Early D/A project at Teton Pines - Photo Vincent R. Lee

Not only was D/A back in the big time, but some major changes had brightened my life outside the office. I'd found a new soul-mate and, in '83, remarried. Nancy Goodman was the smart, beautiful and talented owner of the Soap Opera laundromat where I'd been taking my 'bachelor' wash for several years. Like me, she'd recently ended a relationship and we began sharing our stories over lunch. A dancer and riding enthusiast, she had several horses with which she regularly participated in eventing and jumping competitions. On top of that, like me she had also taught at two Outward Bound schools. With lots in common, her stories were a good match for mine and one thing soon led to another, and then to love.

Nancy Goodman Lee - Photo Vincent R. Lee

We moved in together, sometimes at the Granary and at other times in her snug, self-built log cabin off the Teton Village road. In time, we together bought the Granary property, re-remodeled the old building into a funky but wonderfully livable two-person home upstairs and added a new D/A office in the old HCW space down below. A major benefit of the deal was that it came with the old ranch barn on the adjacent hilltop and five acres of irrigated pasture for Nancy's horses. Adding stalls, a paddock, fencing and a tack room we ended up with a tidy little horse outfit we christened "Red Barn Ranch," and began what at last count is 37 years of living happily ever after. Eventually selling the Soap Opera, she also added her cabin to the ever-expanding Jackson Hole rental market and refocused her time on her horses and dance.

Yet another seismic shift turned my life in an entirely new direction about the same time and Nancy was a big part of it. By the time we got together, HCW had about run its course. Despite the turmoil in my personal life, the climbing school had flourished all through the 70s and early 80s. I had led more than 40 backcountry mountaineering expeditions worldwide, exposed scores of clients to the joys of the Alpine world and summited hundreds of technical peaks at home and abroad. I no longer wanted to be away from home. The twins were grown and doing well out on their own, my youngest son Chris was headed to college, studying architecture, and I was ready for something new.

It happened out of the blue. As mentioned earlier, explorer Gene Savoy's book, Antisuyo, had inspired in me the idea of looking for lost cities in the cloud forests of the Peruvian Andes. It seemed an activity that combined the two things I most enjoyed, architecture and trekking through the high country. Best of all, it was one Nancy and I could share. She'd been a Peace Corps volunteer in Peru back in the 60s and couldn't wait to return! How it all unfolded is described in another of my books, Forgotten Vilcabamba, Final Strong-hold of the Incas. Our first trip, to Cuzco in 1982, was dubbed the Sixpac Manco Expedition for reasons explained in the book, and not only the idea, but the name caught on and stuck. In June of 2019, at ages 79 and 80, she and I completed Sixpac Manco XXVI in the highlands of Peru's remote Cordillera Vilcabamba.

Explorer Gene Savoy (left) and Explorer Vince

Lee in Peru (right) - Photos Unknown and Vincent R. Lee

Despite all of these life-changing developments, one fact remained through it all: I was still making my living as a small-town architect and I needed help again to keep up with the ever-expanding work-load. This time, my choice of a new associate was easy. Chris was nearly done with his architecture program and began helping me in the office especially in the summer months when Nancy and I were off exploring in the Andes. By the late 80s, the days of modest homes for average people were winding down. Chris handled those that turned up, developing his own clientele in the process, but land and construction costs had become so outrageous, fewer people with limited budgets could afford to build. That side of the market moved over Teton Pass to Driggs, Idaho, or down the Snake River Canyon to the crossroads at Alpine Junction, in the next county south. Jackson

Hole was becoming the destination of the mega-wealthy and, as such, was 'architect heaven.' Well-heeled clients were lined up awaiting service. Building contractors were requiring 'retainers' to hold their places in line. The evidence of all of that was apparent in the hundred-plus new practitioners who'd followed Corbett, Morgan and me into the field over the twenty years since I'd settled into the "Last of the Old West."

Expanded Jackson Hole Airport, Grand Teton Park beyond -
Photo Unknown

Not only that, but the airport was now the largest in Wyoming, yearly accommodating ever more flights of bigger and bigger jets from multiple airlines and cities. Noise had become an issue, as planes zoomed in over the Park on final approach. Highway traffic ballooned on all three approaches to the valley, fed by expanding tourism and commuters from the new bedroom communities beyond Jackson. Vacationers, second homeowners and local construction traffic in and out of a myriad of new building sites clogged streets in town. Parking spaces vanished, taxes climbed, prices skyrocketed, but business was great! Jackson built out, then up and began leaking west and south out into the county. Wilson and Teton Village swelled against neighboring Forest Service and private lands. The rich and famous bought entire ranches as private hideaways. Presidents came to visit. The first George Bush had the Secret Service close off streets as his entourage passed through town. In contrast, Bill Clinton stopped everywhere to shake hands, buying lemonades for his entire crew as they passed a stand run by two little girls. The "New West" took hold, as arriving residents donned pricey cowboy boots and Stetson hats and their wives sported Indian jewelry. Gone were the "two-year rule" and being known by the "look in your eye." According to the Chamber of Commerce, Jackson Hole had now morphed into "The Last and Best of the Old West."

D/A, meanwhile, was getting more than its share of the truly great residential commissions flooding into the valley. We'd been around a long time, hadn't screwed up and had the confidence of both realtors and builders, the people new arrivals generally sought out first. The results were some interesting and rewarding projects. Among these were a few that I'm especially proud of. One, the 'Treehouse,' gave me a chance to have another crack at the cancelled NCOBS project that I'd done for my master's thesis at Princeton. The site was on a steep, wooded slope above a hundred-foot cliff down to the flood plain of the Snake. The idea was to perch the house out over the brink of the drop-off to maximize the panoramic views of the Tetons across the river. As with the North Carolina site, access limitations ruled out conventional construction, so my design again utilized big equilateral trusses fashioned from small, easily handled members. Solar clerestory windows heated the north-facing interior and a long stair-way, covered against winter snows, led to a bridge between the garage and house. The owners, both young and athletic, loved the place and so do I.

Treehouse with exposed timber-truss construction - Photos
Vincent R. Lee

It was during this period that I fell in love with stone, much as I earlier had with logs. Most of the former world we see today survives because it was built by masons skillfully using this material, nearly impervious to time and weather. Nowadays, the labor cost is too expensive for most budgets, but I was primed to design a stone house, just waiting for the right clients to come along. Finally, they did. Their site was on a lake with stunning Teton views above a Teton Pines fairway and they wanted something special. I ran the Three Little Pigs story by them and suggested building a house of stone. They loved the idea and two years later we christened the result with a bottle of pricey champagne against a big corner quoin at the front entry. Inside, the vaulted roof above the Great Hall was supported by timber framed 'hammer beam' trusses, adding to its vaguely medieval character. I was and remain proud of it. Years later, a friend from London visiting us in Cortez saw drawings and photos of the house and though he admired the design, characterized it a "Wyoming architect's version of an English manor house," i.e. not quite the real thing.

Timber-framed stone "Manor House" in the Rockies - Photos
Roger Wade and Vincent R. Lee

The owners brought in an interior decorator to do the architecture justice. Some of my fellow practitioners resented other designers meddling with their creations, but I loved it. They almost always did a better job than I would've done and saved me endless hours going through tile samples and color chips. Among other designer touches that might not have occurred to me here was a huge, hand carved medieval fireplace surround, flown in from Italy. At first, they loved the house. The decorator stayed on staff, setting up the entire place for whatever holiday was coming: Fourth of July, Halloween, Thanksgiving, Christmas, Valentine's Day, St. Patty's, all of them. Neither being skiers, though, the owners' extended visits were in summertime. Much as I'd like to report that they live there still, thwarting the huffing and puffing of the "big, bad wolf," it was not to be. The couple's actual home was in Florida and they couldn't imagine a house without air conditioning, even though the annual mean temperature in Jackson Hole is only 7.5 degrees above freezing! On top of that, lady of the house was a former beauty queen and quickly noticed the dry, high altitude air was drying her skin. My engineers had anticipated the former, but not the latter, so a major humidification retrofit was added to the AC system almost immediately. The upshot was that both were turned on "high" all summer long and icicles constantly dripped from the air vents. We never found a way to fix the problem and they soon sold the house, returning to friendlier climes.

The new owners turned off the AC and had a big, icicle-free open house. The design was definitely a crowd-pleaser and caught the attention of all, including the huge real estate 'community' and even the local newspaper. The paper's editor, Mike Sellette, even decided to run a feature about the many grand homes going up all over the valley and interviewed a bunch of us local architects, including me. Asked if all the big money being spent was producing lots of great architecture, I honestly answered, "not necessarily," and witlessly added, "the fees are nice, though." The next day's headline read: LEE: THE FEES ARE NICE! Uh Oh, gotta be a bit more careful talking to the press! I thought. Not long thereafter, one of my favorite clients, who co-owned an especially prestigious restaurant back east, asked to pay my fees in cash. Unsure quite why, I cautiously declined the offer and he agreed to and did pay with cashier checks instead. Several months after the project was done two 'men in black' showed up at my office, one asking, "have any of your recent clients paid your fees mostly or entirely with cash?" No names were mentioned. Caution paid off. "No sir, can't say that they did!" I answered, relieved not to be named "co-conspirator" in a possible IRS investigation.

One of a number of D/A designed CEO "getaways" - Photo
Roger Wade

All through the 80s and 90s, I did second, third and fourth homes for CEOs and Board Chairmen of huge, multi-national corporations. A varied, interesting group, they were connected to and prominent in the larger world beyond the narrow confines of Jackson Hole and Wyoming. Their projects were always challenging, but they presented unique problems as well. One flew into Jackson for a mid-winter meeting about our plans for his large house, scheduled for construction that spring. Weather delayed his flight and when he didn't show up, I had to leave for another conference in town. This was pre-cel-phone, of course, so I left him a note. Returning an hour later, I found him sitting in the snow outside the granary in his city shoes, holding his bleeding forehead, having slipped in the snow and hit it on the roof overhang. He was unable to get up. Fully expecting to be canned on the spot, I administered first aid and poured several shots of Cour-voisier once inside, and we soldiered on with the design. An alto-gether different problem came up now and then with such important and powerful clients, again including this one. A provision in the standard American Institute of Architects contract form that stated that: "The Architect was to be an impartial mediator resolving disputes between the Contractor and the Client." The latter were the ones paying my fees, however, and many understandably thought I should take their sides no matter what. They weren't happy when I didn't.

The following spring, we decided to invite several local contractors to submit competitive bids for his pricey project. Two of the resulting proposals were quite close, suggesting that they were both legitimate prices. The third was double the other two but presented in a much fancier format. I called his office back East and filled him in on the results. He responded that the high bidder's proposal was so impressive, he wanted to award him the job and then talk him down to the lower figures. "That's how we do it back here," he said. I knew I had a big problem. "Out here, all three of them are going to tell you to shove it!" I replied. He insisted, and I actually had to fly back there to settle the matter. "An invitational bid opening," I told him, "is like a card game. If you ask players to the table, the pot goes to the best hand." When I explained that if the pot, his house in this case, ended up going to somebody else, the word would soon get around that Lee was running a crooked game, and no one would show up next time. I was terrified, but I said I'd have to quit rather than allow that to happen. He shouted, "Why that's blackmail!" but that he understood and eventually relented. The low bidder, my old friend Les Weber, won and did a beautiful job but spent even more than the high bidder had quoted due to client embellishment of the project throughout construction, not an uncommon occurrence.

Les and I did a number of fine homes together over the years, developing a relationship uncommon between most architects and contractors. He had an unusually acute sense of design and quickly caught on to the aesthetic result I was after. In lieu of the pages of drawings generally needed to convey the details important to the project concept, we would work problems out on the job sites, often drawing solutions on lumber scraps and handing them to the carpenters. It was a satisfying collaboration for us both and quite the opposite of the animosity that characterizes too many projects. He shared my love of beautifully crafted log work and we often rendered the genre in new and interesting ways. Gone were the days of the modest log 'cabins' of just a few years earlier. The new clients often wanted full-on palaces with accommodations for multiple house guests and great rooms appropriate for large gatherings of cocktail and dinner invitees, commercial-scaled kitchens and laundries, game rooms, wine cellars, home theaters and caretaker apartments above 5-car garages. While we did some of those, we preferred clients with understated desires for comfortable, but not opulent, western homes.

One such home with which we were especially pleased -
Photos Roger Wade

ANOTHER WEBER JOB was for the head of a big family-owned international corporation headquartered in New York and Paris. The house was a gorgeous log lodge on the mountainside between Teton Pass and the Village. Upon completion, the family patriarch came to visit from France and loved the design. Shortly thereafter, I was climbing in the Alps and decided to go to Paris and look him up. Naively, dressed in a T-shirt and jeans, I strolled down the Champs-Élysée toward the address my client had given me for the corporate offices. Suddenly, there it was! A shining new high-rise tower just outside the height-restricted zone with the family crest emblazoned above the monumental entry. In the lobby, two uniformed guards sporting Uzis took one look and asked who the hell I was and why I was there. I gave my name and said that I wanted to meet their boss, explaining that he'd know who I was. They both laughed but called upstairs to humor me.

Design Associates, Architects

Early sketch of the mountainside lodge - Image Vincent R. Lee

Their smirks disappeared when the call was connected, and they were told the patrón would be right down. He emerged from the elevator quite a pleasant and distinguished gentleman straight from central casting as a European aristocrat, Armani suit, coiffed white mane, ascot and all. He had just moved into his new building and, proud that he'd had a major hand in its design, spent the afternoon showing me around.

The 80s and 90s were heady times for a small-town architect in Jackson Hole. The wealthy were pouring in, many looking for expressions of their success with which to dazzle their out-of-town, cocktail party and dinner guests. The answer I'd given to Mike Sellette that big money doesn't necessarily mean great architecture was proving to be true. As the houses became larger and more opulent, many became showplaces rather than homes. I tried to avoid it in my own work, but in some of the monstrosities being built it was hard to find a single comfortable room unless you were entertaining thirty friends. Even the log construction I'd thought so 'honest' was being corrupted by the addition of hidden steel to accomplish structural feats not possible with even the largest logs. Contrarily, some macho clients demanded giant 24" wall logs for the most modest structures, turning whole projects into architectural cartoons. None of this posturing had anything to do with architecture. It was all just expensive stagecraft.

Toward the end of the 90s, a number of other factors came together suggesting that it might be time to hang up my T-square. I'd been at it for thirty years and hours hunched over a drafting table were losing the appeal they'd once had. Computer Assisted Drafting, or CAD, was fast coming online anyway, changing the entire process of doing the drawings I had so enjoyed crafting by hand. My son Chris, now working full time, ordered a new program called Archicad 1.0 that revolutionized even the architectural design process. It was aimed specifically at architects and automatically created construction documents based on an ongoing, 3-dimensional screen model of the evolving design. He quickly became a digital wizard and continues using it today, but at level 23.0, leading an expanded and vibrant D/A more technologically sophisticated than anything I'd ever imagined. Before turning the firm over to him, I'd made a half-hearted attempt to learn the futuristic ropes, but kept falling back on my old, familiar ways. Drawing lines with a pencil was not only easier, but more satisfying to a dinosaur like me than learning, and then having to remember all the tricks of doing it electronically.

Dealing with the increasingly Byzantine county permitting process, for which I had been an early advocate was also starting to wear on me. Most of my time, it seemed, went into accommodating my designs to a myriad of ever-changing code requirements, plan reviewers and site inspectors. It was no fun anymore. A flap that arose with one of my wealthy clients about this time illustrates the point. CEO of one of Hollywood's major film studios, he and his wife asked me to design a plush guest house for their many important visitors. The county rules limited the square footage of such structures to "ten percent of the area of the principle residence," in this case ten thousand square feet. With this in mind, I came up with a handsome little one thousand square-foot cottage, did all the drawings and submitted them to the Planning Department. Shortly thereafter, the County Planner called to reject my submission on the grounds that it was "too big." I protested that it was precisely ten percent of the main house. "Did you include the garage?" she asked. "Of course," I said, there being no language in the rule suggesting otherwise. "We exclude garage areas," she replied. When I noted no such exclusion in the written text, she admitted that it was just an "office policy!" How the hell was I supposed to know that? I solved the problem, but it was a stressful negotiation.

The final blow came in the most unlikely of places, Easter Island. Nancy and I were participating in a NOVA TV production there, dealing with methods for moving and erecting the giant stone statues, called moai, for which the island is famous. At one point during the filming, an islander was injured and needed medical care. Not being on camera just then, I offered to take him to the tiny medical clinic then the only hospital for thousands of kilometers in any direction. Nancy and I loaded him into the Suzuki Samurai we'd been loaned during the shoot and sped off across the island. Our patient wasn't badly hurt and received the first aid treatment and stitches he needed from the clinic's lone doctor and nurse, using just the few basic supplies available. What if he'd been near mortally wounded or seriously ill? we wondered. What then? Without a plane ticket to Tahiti or Santiago Chile, both about 2500 air miles away, he'd be out of luck. It struck me that for the money my clients routinely spent just furnishing their second, third and sometimes fourth homes in Jackson Hole, the Rapanui islanders could have had a decent, well equipped hospital. Hard to imagine, I know, but for the first time in my career it dawned on me that what I was doing was not only less fun than it used to be, but a little bit crazy and maybe even shameful.

Re-erected Easter Island moai, My wife Nancy at lower right - Photo Unknown

CHAPTER 8
SAVING THE GOOSE

Rewinding our tale back to where we started, in the Jackson Hole of 1968, a whole other story was set to unfold with some of the same characters, myself included, but a nearly opposite theme. Even then, there was a small clutch of environmental visionaries who foresaw what the future held for the pristine valley I had been so attracted to. The new ski area wasn't yet online, and no one knew whether it would be a success. The brisk but brief two-month Yellowstone tourist season was still the backbone of the local economy. The wild beauty and "old west" spirit of the place were understood by almost everyone to be the geese that had always reliably laid the "golden eggs" that kept everything going.

Old time Jackson Hole, hay meadows, woods and peaks -
Photo Irjalina Paavonperan

No one wanted to risk killing those geese, nor did anyone including me imagine that they were in danger. The new ski resort, even if successful, seemed to everyone just one more possible source of tourist money, always welcomed in the past. As expected, the project got off to an underwhelming start, plagued by sketchy finances and inconvenient early travel access for prospective skiers. Even so, new winter dollars began to flow, and many valley residents quickly latched onto the contrary notion that there might somehow be a way to capitalize on a potential off-season bonanza and thus "have their cake and eat it too." There had long been skeptical old school conservationists in the valley, but this initially subtle, but spreading attitude shift, occurring almost exactly as I arrived in the valley, inspired a new environmental activism locally mimicking that then underway nation-wide.

Leading the charge were two local naturalists, Verne Huser and Keith Becker. Far from having their credentials, I nevertheless shared their concerns and preservationist passions from day one. Having left the crowded East and gravitated to the wilds of the mountain West, the last thing I wanted was to see them spoiled by the same forces I'd just left behind. No contradiction between that attitude and my aspirations as an architect ever occurred to me. My intention was to design buildings that celebrated rather than despoiled Nature, and besides, I'd be barely nibbling at the cake, or so I thought. Meanwhile, the first Earth Day was just around the corner and a bunch of us would-be tree huggers formed a group to join in the world-wide kick-off of a whole new environmental awareness. We organized ourselves as the Jackson Hole Environmental Action Society or ENACT for short. Early in 1970, I was elected to be its first president and thus began my auxiliary career as a "loud-mouthed, new-comer, Eastern radical" bent on destroying the age-old Wyoming Way of Life, or so my detractors thought.

Beginning next week, Design Associates of Wilson will make this space available for the continuing publication of notices, comments messages and photographs aimed at arousing public awareness, concern and action regarding matters affecting the quality of the physical environment which we all share.

Suggestions as to content are invited and will be welcomed from any responsible source. Interested individuals or organizations should submit such material to D/A at least one week in advance of desired publication.

Weekly D/A sponsored environmental posts in the Jackson
newspaper announcing formation of ENACT. (Note the
prescient border beginning at lower left, starting with all trees,
adding a few people, then adding cars and ending with all
people and cars.)

John Morgan and his partners gave ENACT the use of the abandoned Skyline Ranch granary, that was to figure so prominently in
my own Jackson Hole future, as a rent-free 'headquarters.' Filled with
grain dust and spiders, it offered a covered place to meet, but not
much more. This became especially evident during our Earth Day
planning sessions through the winter of '69-'70. Without heat or light
other than flashlights, meetings tended to be short and often relocated
to the Stagecoach Bar in Wilson. Still, the big day arrived, and we
were ready. A badly needed roadside trash pickup had been decided as
a way to involve lots of people and get them excited. Local businesses
donated plastic bags, the Sheriff's Department directed traffic and the
county agreed to dispose of the trash. The day dawned clear and cold,
as was then typical of April, but snow was beginning to recede from

the roadsides and expose enough trash there to make the whole project worthwhile.

A large turnout surprised us a bit, since the 'booster' crowd, ever promoting development, had painted ENACT as a subversive organization from day one. Maybe cleaning up the roadsides was widely seen as a good idea and one not likely to get anyone unintentionally pegged as an 'environmentalist.' For whatever reason, a cross-section of Jackson Hole took part, including more than a few developers and lots of others focused more on local economic opportunity than unspoiled nature, perhaps hoping to soften their public images. My route was along state Highway 22, the road connecting the town of Jackson with Wilson, Teton Pass and points beyond in Idaho. Just west of where Highway 390, the dead-end road to fledgling Teton Village turned off to the north, my personal pickup area crossed a marshy bog, favored most winters by moose escaping the deep snow elsewhere, atop a causeway of snow-free boulders basking in the weak spring sunshine.

As one of the organizers, I was involved in assigning others to their respective areas, making sure that everyone had plastic bags and tending to all the other details needed to get things going. I wasn't paying much attention to the patch of highway margin I'd reserved for myself and by the time I got there to begin work, the sun had been on the boulders long enough to warm them up. The slope off the roadside was about twenty feet long down to the swamp and fairly steep, scattered with years of accumulated beer cans and other junk, so at least it wasn't going to be a boring, unsatisfying day of plodding along, hour after hour without finding or accomplishing much.

WHO PLANTS
ROADSIDE SNOW LILIES?

Two more D/A posts before the 1970 roadside trash pickup

Boredom, it turned out, was not going to be a big problem. Stepping off the hardtop onto the boulders focused on my first treasure, an old rusty muffler with several feet of tailpipe attached, I began noticing something soft and gooey underfoot and started paying more attention to the rocks, it seemed they were all moving. What the hell? Looking closer, they were covered with tiny snakes, zillions of them! Yikes! It was the scene from Ford's Raiders, right there on Highway 22 and I was completely surrounded! They were crawling all over my boots, inches from my socks and legs. Momentarily terrified, I found getting back up to the road without putting my hands among the snakes tricky, given the slippery footholds, but I did it double-time. Needless to say, that part of the roadside didn't get picked up. Thinking back, I guess you could call it a weird sort of Earth Day celebration of Nature's abundance. Years later, I saw a TV special documenting the bizarre fact that every so often, common grass snakes do that, overproducing unimaginable numbers of mini offspring, soon to be gobbled up by every bird and critter in the neighborhood.

A year or so into the job, an incident during one of our meetings began to give me pause about environmental activism. It was the dead of a hard '71-'72 winter and we had shunned the granary and gathered instead at the Heidelberg restaurant, part-way up Teton Pass. I was seated next to a large plate glass window outside of which was a giant snowdrift nearly up to the second story sill. I don't recall the details, but the Ford Motor Company had committed some unforgivable offense against the planet and our membership was irately up in arms. Something had to be done! On and on went the repetitive discussion until, finally, I called for a motion. With an entirely straight face, one of our more naive, other-worldly members called for shutting down the Ford Motor Company from our base right there in Wilson, Wyoming. As the motion was not only seconded, but passed, I found myself looking out the window, wondering how badly I'd be cut and injured during a sudden escape through the glass into the hopefully cushioning snowbank and on out into the frozen night.

Spring brought another kind of awakening in my new role as a 'public figure.' Lake Tahoe, California, was at the time experiencing many of the very same growth challenges as we anticipated in Jackson Hole, so we decided to sponsor a public forum bringing together people with varying opinions about runaway development in both places. Among the invitees was Roy Peck, a Republican state representative from nearby Riverton, who was a well know promoter in Wyoming affairs. He was first up, so I took a few minutes to get acquainted before opening the forum. Roy was well aware of ENACT and all smiles about our efforts on behalf of Nature. He said the rest of the state was behind me and he wished me luck. Wow! I hardly expected that and warmly introduced him to the audience as the first speaker. He took the podium, turned to me and said, "I want to thank my good friend, Vince Lee, a newly arrived East Coast architect that thinks he knows better than we do how we should run Wyoming!" and drawing chuckles from the crowd. Ah, politics! I was starting to learn.

My term at the helm of ENACT was about up and the following year found me Acting Director of another group, the Friends of Jackson Hole, focused on adoption of a first-ever Master Plan for the Valley as well as the zoning ordinances needed to bring about its goals. OMG! The only thing worse than planning was the metric system. Both were communist tricks designed to undermine the Republic, according to our booster-minded opponents. Anyone in favor of planning was an enemy of all things Jackson Hole, Wyoming and American! The problem was that any honest and impartial look at the mounting growth pressures all over the valley made it clear to the reasonable that something had to be done, and quick, if we weren't soon to lose the development war.

Jon Roush, Northwest Regional Director for The Nature Conservancy arrived with a grant to help pay for a planner. The County Commissioners, after much debate, voted two to one to accept the money, hire someone and worry later about possibly enacting the results into law. Larry Livingston, fresh from a successful growth control campaign in Petaluma, California, was chosen to do the work. Recall that this was before computers were in anything like wide scale private use. Livingston planned to analyze the valley and its resources using a clever method recently pioneered by the Scottish planner Ian McHarg, using transparent plastic map overlays showing the locations and extent of various key features in different colors. Combining two or more such sheets over a light table thus showed high value or high impact areas at a glance and simplified the process of knowing what was where.

"IT CAN'T HAPPEN HERE!"

BUT IT HAS............

CONGRATULATIONS
TO JACKSON ON ITS
NEW MASTER PLAN

NEXT: THE COUNTY

More D/A rabble rousing in support of the new Master Plan

To assure that local ideas, concerns and values would guide Livingston's work, a County Planning Study Group was appointed in 1976 and I was one of a wide range of members. The Commissioners election that fall, however, was contested by opponents of the entire process. Art Brown, one of the two aye votes on the three-man board, and the realtor who'd sold me my place on Wenzel Lane, decided not the run for reelection. Uh oh. That gave the boosters the chance to put their own man in there and kill the whole deal. They ran Peter Hansen, son of Senator Cliff Hansen, a prominent local rancher and former Governor. They were Republicans, of course, and the Democrats, a distinct minority, chose Muffy Moore, former wife of Barry Corbet, one of the successful 1963 American Mount Everest climbers, to run against him. The glass ceiling was feared firmly in place. Most thought Hansen would win, killing any chance Livingston's work would go anywhere. The only way to avoid that outcome might be by running an independent, me, they thought, to mobilize the enviro vote. I, meanwhile, had been off guiding in the nearby Wind River

Mountains and got home to find the planning proponents in an uproar. Would I run? Like a dummy, I agreed. But what about Muffy? We couldn't split the vote on our side. She had to get out of the race, and it was up to me to make that happen.

Ever since Roy Peck had dissed me at the Lake Tahoe forum, I'd been skeptical of politics. What was I thinking? Immediately, Pete's angry side of town became my sworn enemies and even my own friends started questioning my positions on every issue imaginable. One day into the contest and I was already uncomfortable! I didn't know Muffy well but decided to find out what she thought over lunch at the upscale Alpenhof restaurant out at the Village. We chatted around the campaign for awhile, enjoying the meal, drinking wine and sizing one another up. It was fun. I don't know what she thought of me, the interloper, but I was totally impressed by her obvious intelligence and grasp of County issues. I liked her. She was the perfect candidate. I wanted to vote for her! After several rounds, we were confronted by a small phalanx of Republican big shots from over in town. They disingenuously congratulated me on entering the contest but said there was no need. Muffy would do just fine and I could only spoil her chances. As they left, I asked her what she thought. "They're more scared of you than me, but I'll show those SOBs!" I ended my candidacy that very night without having said or done much of anything. Mike Sellette wrote in the Jackson Hole News the next day that mine was the "cleanest campaign" he'd ever seen!

1976 Campaign add

Fallout was immediate. "What the hell was I doing?" complained my friends. It was too late to put someone else in the race to replace me, so they feared I had just handed the valley's fate over to the opposition, and maybe they were right. With considerable trepidation, I awaited the election day results, but good karma prevailed! Moore unexpectedly cleaned Hansen's clock and went on to become one of the county's best Commissioners for the next six years. Vince Lee was, if not a hero, at least not a villain. With two aye votes safely restored, the process went on with renewed vigor. Committee meetings went on through the winter, with draft after draft of a proposed document hashed over, sent back to California, revised and submitted anew. Finally, after months of haggling with nearly everyone in the county, in late '77 Livingston delivered a final product to the Commissioners. Their vote was to determine the future of Jackson Hole. The issue would be decided at their December meeting.

The public was well represented, both the yeas and the nays being out in force. As one of the staunchest advocates, I was in the hearing room. Max May, an old-time conservative was a guaranteed nay. Bill Ashley, whose house I'd designed, was a sure yea, as was newly seated Moore. Many valley building contractors had ringed the courthouse with their backhoes and dump trucks in protest. There was electricity in the air. Finally, after a bit of speechifying, the question was called and by a two to one vote the county had its first Comprehensive Plan. A howl arose among the opponents, many of whom would eventually be enriched by the county's commitment to a more orderly, thoughtfully planned future.

As I walked out into the picket line, Don Phillips a stone- mason who'd done lots of my block foundations and a key protest leader, put his beefy arm over my shoulder and shouted into my ear, "You'll live to regret this, Vince!" For the next twenty years, I thought of Don every single time I walked into the endlessly growing Teton County Planning Department, eventually wondering if he might have been right. Even Livingston, in later life, became disillusioned with planning in general and many of his own projects in particular. Forcing people to forego doing what they really want to or to do what they'd rather not, turns everyone into a petty crook, looking for ways around the rules. Plugging these leaks soon turns the play book into the IRS Code, so voluminous and complicated that even its administrators can't fairly apply it across the board. And, worst of all, in the end, all it seems to do is tidy up the urbanization of the place you're trying to preserve.

It was with reservations like these in mind that I began shifting my energies away from activism and toward land preservation. The

Conservancy's Roush had also introduced the then new concept of 'conservation easements' to the valley, another communist trick, but one that paid something, at least, for desired development constraints. I liked the idea a lot. The ranchers had said all along, "If you want to 'save' my place, all you gotta do is buy it!" Despite my enviro leanings, I had to agree. Regulating away people's property rights was never going to get the job done. So it was that in 1973, I was appointed local agent for the Nature Conservancy and D/A became the local TNC office. Several long-time conservation-minded landowners, including John Morgan, his wife Georgie and his Skyline Ranch partners stepped up to the plate and donated easements, receiving tax breaks for their generosity, fairly attractive in those days because the tax rates were much higher than now. When the sky didn't fall, others became interested and a whole other preservation regime began to take root. TNC, just then moving its focus into a larger, world-wide theater, urged us locals to form our own Jackson Hole Land Trust to continue and manage the program, which in 1980, we did. Jean Hocker, my friend Phil's wife, and Story Clark, from one of the valley's more conservation-minded ranch families, looked into other local and regional land preservation groups then forming nation-wide and put together a proposal for one to focus specifically on Jackson Hole. Its goals were the protection of the remaining "scenic open spaces, wildlife and traditional ranching character" in the valley. I was one of the founding board members and served for the next sixteen years, including a term as JHLT's second president following Bill Ashley, it's first. Both of us enjoyed the invaluable assistance of Jean Hocker, the Land Trust's first Executive Director. Much of the group's later success was due to her leadership.

CHAPTER 9
HIGH PLACED FRIENDS

A s all of this local environmental activity gained traction in the 1970s, similar citizen groups were forming elsewhere in Wyoming. This was seen as threatening by the development-friendly boosters and conservative Republican administrators over in Cheyenne. The rest of the state had long regarded Teton County as a stepchild, not quite part of the real Wyoming. Just read any of C J Box's macho Wyoming novels. Jealous of its world-class attractions and resulting prosperity, they were suspicious of the 'new' ideas that often leaked eastward over the passes and out of the mountains, onto the wind-swept eastern plains. In time, Jackson Hole came to be called the "California of Wyoming," and though more or less true, it wasn't meant as a compliment.

Into this chauvinistic atmosphere came the National Environmental Policy Act (NEPA) of 1970. Among other provisions, it gave control of air, land and water protection to the federal government unless individual states created their own agencies to do so with standards at least as high. The feds already owned almost half of the state and the very idea they might take control over what happened on the rest was unthinkable! Stan Hathaway, the sitting right-wing Governor, reluctantly began urging his like-minded legislators to get busy on an act of their own to head off the feds. One of his pet projects was to industrialize the state east of the Rockies. The problem was lack of water there and he proposed to dam the pristine upper Green River, a major headwater tributary of the Colorado, and pump the water eastward over the continental divide. As the legislature considered the idea, a bunch of us valley opponents descended on the capital in Cheyenne to testify, typically identifying ourselves as, "so and so, from Wilson, Wyoming." After several of us had stepped up, legislators were heard mumbling, "where the hell is Wilson, Wyoming?" The measure eventually failed, but Hathaway wasn't done.

Republican Governor Stan Hathaway - Photo Unknown

IN 1973, the Wyoming Environmental Quality Act was signed into law. Among other things, it established three Advisory Boards to oversee Air and Water quality respectively as well as Land Reclamation by the surface mining industry. These Boards were to bring matters of concern to the attention of a 7-member, rule-making Environmental Quality Council. Both Board and Council members were to be appointed by the governor. In Cheyenne, the whole idea was to foil the feds, since grazing, logging, mining, oil and gas drilling and other such industries were the lifeblood of the state. The last thing the status-quo crowd wanted was a bunch of panty-waist eastern tree-huggers meddling in these all-American, tax producing enterprises. Extractive industry paid the bills, such that no state income taxes were levied. "Wyoming people were independent, self reliant pioneers who could take care of themselves without any damned help from Washington," as the politicians saw it. A contemporary article in the New York Times nevertheless pointed out that fully a quarter of the state's population worked for government, one way or another, and for every buck paid by Wyomingites to the feds, they got back $1.30 in benefits. The author, an Englishman writing in New York where the same figure was less than $.90, went on to say that he was thinking of "moving out there," as tax-averse out-of-state billionaires have been doing ever since.

But I digress. Hathaway's problem was that he had to fill the seats on the Council and Advisory Boards with his cronies without it looking too much like a fix. Who to choose? That's where I entered the picture. Unbeknownst to me, all of my local subversive activity had not gone unnoticed over in Cheyenne. In fact, I quite unexpectedly ran into the Governor at a local fund raiser about that time and introduced myself. Shaking my hand, he said, "Still up to the same tricks, Mr. Lee?" Whoa! What tricks? At a loss for anything else to say, I said "More so than ever, Governor." Not long thereafter came a brief letter from Hathaway's Office appointing me to the newly formed Air Quality Advisory Board in Cheyenne. Clearly, I was to be the token environmentalist on the five-person committee. Hugh "Bigfoot" Binford, Manager of the sprawling Sinclair Oil Refinery down in

Rawlins, and long-time Republican operative in Wyoming was appointed Chairman. Standing well over six feet, with size fifteen shoes, he was an imposing figure. The other three members were 'good ole boy' ranchers from out in the high plains. None of them seemed especially interested in the job, so they elected me Co-Chairman at our first meeting.

We were to be aided in our efforts by a new, full-time Air Quality Administrator named Randolph Wood, who took the job very seriously indeed. The issues before us were all major industrial problems, a long way from the parochial concerns of Jackson Hole, and I immediately enjoyed the work. The first of two biggies Randy put on our agenda was a proposed new permit system requiring any facility emitting pollutants to identify them and estimate their magnitude before being allowed to continue or begin operations. The second was a sweeping new rule requiring sulfur dioxide "scrubbers" on the stacks of any facility emitting that gas into the atmosphere. It was a response to the 'acid rain' problem being increasingly detected and objected to in the downwind states. In short, the first would identify who was emitting what, and how much. The second would make them fix the worst of it. Both would strongly affect the existing coal-fired power plants in the state and the many then being planned for the future.

Unless you were a) the governor, b) a Republican, c) in the coal mining or power generation business or d) any other industry that emitted anything, it was a no-brainer. Of course, we should begin regulating air pollution! We debated both proposals at length. As a state employee, Randy feigned neutrality, but was clearly in favor of both. Numerous industry representatives claimed we would, "put them out of business!" and "destroy the state's entire economy!" if we dared to recommended either one. Interestingly, over drinks at the Hitching Post bar long after the meetings adjourned and the minutes were closed and mics turned off, they would say, "we don't give a damn what the rules are so long as our competitors have to abide by the same ones!" That struck me a legitimate argument, since they were up against outfits from Montana, Ohio, West Virginia and other places with different laws. On the other hand, the federal standards set a baseline applicable to all. The only publicly favorable voice came from the Powder River Basin Resource Council, a state-wide enviro group pointing out that various other states had already adopted similar rules without undue disruption.

Bigfoot, ever the larger-than-life, important, powerful fellow with "places to go and people to see," especially in Washington, DC, vigorously opposed both, but often missed our quarterly meetings, leaving me with the gavel. Having heard testimony from everyone with a stake in the issues, and at just such a meeting, I thought maybe it was time to stop talking and decide the matters, something Bigfoot seemed unlikely ever to do. It was a bit risky, since the other three members of the committee had mostly listened carefully to the testimony, expressing neither support nor opposition to the measures. Nevertheless, I asked for motions on both proposals from my colleagues, got them along with seconds and called the questions. Four constituted a quorum, so Bigfoot's absence wasn't a problem. Both recommendations passed four to zip! All three good ole boys turned out to be closet enviros!

The news went overnight all over the state. At last, "Air pollution would be controlled in Wyoming!" the papers said and the public approved. Actually, our decisions still had to be confirmed and acted upon by the Environmental Quality Council before anything happened. Bless them, bolstered by positive public support and despite huge pressure from Hathaway and industry, they agreed with us and passed both measures. At our very next meeting we were summoned over to the Capitol building by Hathaway. The other four of us sat nervously out in the rotunda, staring at the giant stuffed bison there as Bigfoot was escorted into the Governor's office. The acoustics were great. A loud voice echoed from within, "God dammit, Binford, what the hell did you think I made you Chairman for? Can't you control those f---ing people?" Not surprisingly, I served only one term. Binford, too, was canned and went on to run for the US Senate against Alan Simpson in 1977.

SHOOTING FROM THE LIP

THE LIFE OF SENATOR
AL SIMPSON

DONALD LOREN HARDY

A battle of Titans!

As a footnote, I ran into Simpson at the Triangle X Ranch opening in Jackson Hole a year later, and he was worried that Bigfoot's "good environmental record" might cost him the enviro vote. I laughed. "Check our minutes, Alan" I suggested. Binford had always voted "yes" on new pickups for the staff, but "no" on anything remotely related to our committee's stated mission of environmental protection in the public's interest. Simpson followed up, called later to say "thanks" and was elected in 1978, serving until 1997. One result of my ill sought notoriety in both Jackson and Cheyenne was that I got noticed in

Washington as well. In 1975, I was appointed to the National Park Rocky Mountain Regional Advisory Committee as well as a steering committee studying possible changes to the boundaries of Grand Teton Park. Aside from me, the former group consisted of prominent high rollers and politicos from Wyoming, Montana and Colorado. Our quarterly meetings rotated among the region's spectacular Parks and dealt mostly with parochial concessioner problems, not national issues. It was fun, but the whole program was shelved during the Carter Administration as a cost-saving measure. It was during my tenure that Denver was proposed for the 1972 Winter Olympics and soon became controversial due to both economic and environmental impacts experienced by prior Olympic hosts. As an enviro, I was privy to the depth of these concerns, but the other members were shocked when Colorado voters rejected the proposal. For the first time, I realized how remote the rich and powerful could be to what was actually going on.

Concurrently, I was appointed to a local committee to establish a Jackson Hole National Scenic Area to protect the Park boundaries from encroachment and perpetuate the surrounding open ranch lands. One of our big local ranchers, former Governor Cliff Hansen, was now one of our two Wyoming Senators and ranking Republican on the Interior Committee considering the proposal in Washington.

Wyoming Senator Clifford P. Hansen - Painting Michelle
Rushworth

One of Hansen's former staffers, attorney Brent Coonce and I even flew back there in '77 to lobby the resulting Scenic Area Bill, already passed by the House. The tab was estimated at $200 million, but when we ran that by Hansen's party colleague, Oregon Senator Mark Hatfield, he quipped, "It'll be 350 or 400 million before we're done." He would probably have been right or low, given the gold rush that passage of the bill would surely have precipitated among valley landowners. Hansen, for his part, publicly said little one way or the other, his large ranch holdings being squarely in the bull's eye of the lands to be protected. For him and his neighbors, the question was: who would pay more for their acres, the feds or future developers? History has since resoundingly answered that question in favor of the bill's opponents. During our DC visit, Hansen avoided discussing the bill, but at one point confided to Brent and me that, "I always give the voters pictures of myself shaking hands with them. It makes them feel important and they love it! Easy votes!" Sure enough, as we left his office, one of his staffers a bit disappointingly handed us each an 8x10 glossy of ourselves shaking hands with the grinning senator. The bill failed in the Senate. Hansen claimed he'd had nothing to do with it, but that seemed to many, unlikely.

The late '70s saw a brief hiatus in my extra curricular activities aimed at saving the world while I instead endured the "interesting times" recounted earlier. Recall that while I'd been paying the bills running Design Associates, Architects and High Country West, Alpine Adventures, all of that public service found me logging in even more of the time away from home that finally contributed to the 1978 breakup of my marriage. The new decade, though, turned everything around, not only in my life, but in the valley. The Jackson Hole Land Trust, for example, was up and running and starting to catch on. All through the '80s and '90s, it set aside parcel after parcel of open land, 25,000 acres, as I write this, in the valley of Jackson Hole, fully a third of the privately-owned land there. Much of the valley's scenic open space today is due to the success of JHLT's efforts.

An incident toward that end is worth recounting. State Highway 22, again the scene of my Raiders snake encounter, split the hayfields of Hardeman Ranch right down the middle for a half mile before passing through Wilson at the bottom of Teton Pass. Preventing development of those fields was a major JHLT objective in preserving the scenic quality of the West Bank. A deal was struck, and a huge community fund-raiser staged to fund the purchase. It was not only a major financial contribution toward realization of the project, but an unexpectedly popular local event. A large, enthusiastic crowd turned out including not only JHLT supporters, but many residents previously uninvolved in land conservation. An attitude change was afoot. A strong majority was beginning to form around the preservation idea, and the fact that popular families like the Hardemans were being compensated at last for their years of stewardship made a big difference.

Public support, however strong, wasn't nearly enough to

completely close the gap between the buyers and sellers. That came from major donors and the auctioning of three parcels back off the highway, to private owners. To prevent them from spoiling the hard-won scenery, JHLT imposed strict planning and design limits on the three sales, much as the county was doing on residential development elsewhere around the valley. Typically, the rules limited building heights and prevented garish exterior colors or highly reflective surfaces to head off intrusive designs. Ironically, however, one of the parcels was the original ranch headquarters, and included an enormous, 40-foot high, bright red barn with a silver metal roof! It was and remains one of the valley's iconic structures, beloved by everyone in or passing through the valley to this day. We had no choice but to 'grandfather' the barn. So much for the aesthetic limitations I'd supported so enthusiastically for years, I thought. The rules tended to prevent architectural atrocities, but imposed monotony instead, as remains evident to a discerning observer even today. Everything looks pretty much alike. Besides, as noted earlier, I was finding the rules increasingly burdensome. The architect in me found them frustrating and tedious to deal with, but even I had to admit, absent any controls at all, the result would have been chaos.

Since 1975, there had also been big changes over in Cheyenne. Ed Herschler, a Democrat, had replaced Hathaway in the governor's office and the old-line developers were out of power. Despite its usually conservative leanings, Wyoming switched parties now and then due to a strong railroad labor vote down along the Union Pacific spanning the southern edge of the state. Most of the state's few residents lived there as well. Casper, the state's oil-and-gas capital, was the main exception. Herschler was something of a populist, often holding forth in the bar out at the Cheyenne airport. Miners, oilmen, ranchers and cowboys opined there night after night over a drink or two with "good old Ed." While well aware that industry paid the bills, he was a lot more open to taking care of the environment than his predecessor. Out of the blue, in 1985, I got a letter from his office offering me an appointment to the Environmental Quality Council.

My single term on the Air Quality Advisory Board had apparently not been forgotten. By then Nancy and I were settled into married life, further remodeling the old granary into a combination home-office and taking off on month-long expeditions to Peru every summer. In other words, we were happily busy. Still, the appointment was tempting. I saw the Council seat as an opportunity to make a real difference in Wyoming's future and the meetings were only quarterly, so the time commitment didn't seem problematic. Given that the Andean dry season, the best time to be in Peru, fell right between the spring and late summer meeting dates, I accepted. Only later I learned that my name had been suggested to the governor by Jack Pugh, a legislator that I hardly knew at the time, but who graciously contributed the Foreword to this book. A long-time environmental advocate, Jack and his minority of fellow Democrats were finally able, with Herschler's blessings, to get good things done for Wyoming. Jack and I became better acquainted over time and remain friends to this day.

Wyoming Governor Ed Herschler - Photo Caspser Star Tribune

What a group the Council I joined l was! There were seven of us appointed by Herschler, six of us firmly dedicated to the Council's mission of safeguarding environmental quality. The seventh member was an industry representative mandated by the statute and, while often sympathetic, he was typically careful not to offend his bosses. I don't recall who the chairman was when I came onboard, but John Crow, a Yale-trained lawyer from tiny Pinedale was our most eloquent spokesman, frequently interjecting humor into our proceedings. Casper attorney, Dave Park, was his co-comedian, the two of them keeping the rest of us smiling with their endless string of puns and one-liners. Dr. Harold Bergman and Fred Carr were our scientists, Fred a geologist and Harold a science professor at the university in Laramie. Next came John Schiffer, an honest-to-goodness, missing-fingers-rancher from K-C, out on the plains. Finally came me, no longer the token environmentalist, but rather a conservation-comrade-in-arms. We had two jobs: first we reviewed recommendations from the three Advisory Boards, acting on or rejecting them by vote after lengthy public hearings and discussion at our regular meetings. In addition, we individually served as Hearing Officers whenever local public input was sought on the above issues or disputes arose over measures already passed. Public participation was never a problem. In either case, at quarterly Council meetings or contested public hearings, industry people, a lively public and a curious press were always in attendance.

By the time I got there, a lot of regulatory water had flowed over the dam and there were many more disputes than new proposals, so we divied up the numerous contested hearings among ourselves, playing the role of judges. It was fascinating work and fun. Unlike my attorney colleagues, I had to learn courtroom procedure and the rules of evidence. They didn't call the hearings 'contested' for nothing. All the parties were 'lawyered up' and the public wasn't bashful about letting off steam. Having given everyone present her or his time at the microphone, a record was made with which we each presented the results at the next regular Council meeting. Some hearings were so crazy or entertaining that fellow Councilors would show up and join the Hearing Officer just for fun. Most satisfying of all was the fact that we were the deciding body, not just recommending policy. The buck stopped with us and even an unhappy governor couldn't overrule our decisions. He could fail to reappoint us when our four-year terms expired, but that didn't often happen, even when the party in power changed hands. Appointed by Herschler and kept on by Mike Sullivan, also a Democrat, and his successor, Republican Jim Geringer, I served for twelve years, until 1997.

During my time, at least, we six took pretty good care of Wyoming, a state often thought of by industry and outsiders as a sacrifice zone, just a bunch of flat, worthless sagebrush. None of our good work had much impact on Jackson Hole, though, the heart of my story here, with one exception: gravel pits. It doesn't sound like much, I know, but they are found everywhere and are seldom good neighbors. If they are next to land worth millions an acre, big trouble can result. One of most the most bitterly fought cases I judged dealt with an abandoned and flooded pit owned by the Hansen family - yes, Senator Hansen. His son Pete, the unsuccessful Commissioner candidate, had subdivided the land all around the pit and sold it off for serious bucks. Shortly thereafter, Pete told all his happy homeowners that he was reopening the gravel operation. Uh oh! We're talking noise, dust, truck traffic, night lighting, just what his buyers had just built pricey getaways in paradise to get away from. Hansen was a big shot, but so were lots of his opponents.

The more-than-irate landowners brought in their own high-priced, outside legal guns and Hansen hired several local barristers of note to hold them off. Sorting all this out was Vince Lee, small-town architect, part-time mountain guide and well-known commie-environmentalist. No sooner I had convened the hearing than Hansen's people moved to voir dire the Hearing Officer. Having no idea what that meant, I consulted the Council's Executive Director Terri Lorenzon, sitting by my side, and she advised that they thought I would be biased and wanted a chance to prove it. The good news was that I could put it off until after the respective cases were presented, and I so ruled with considerable relief. After opening statements, the arguments went something like this:

Owners: "You didn't say anything about this when you sold us our places."

Hansen: "You didn't ask, and any fool could see there was a pit over there."

Owners: "Yea, but it had obviously been closed and unused for years."

Hansen, " It's my property and I've got a right to open it again if I want to."

Owners, turning to the County Planner, a bureaucrat trying hard to stay out of the middle: "Is this legal? There's gotta be a rule against this sort of thing!"

Abandoned and flooded gravel pit - Photo Unknown

As it turned out, there wasn't, but the less reticent County Engineer, sitting in the back, volunteered that the access road in from the highway had been platted by Hansen himself as a "Subdivision Road," not a "County Road" and the Master Plan said quite clearly that 'industrial' traffic was not permitted on Subdivision Roads. Thus, while Hansen might legally open the pit, there was no clear way to get the machinery in or the gravel out of the site. An uproar ensued. I called a brief recess to calm everyone down. The senator, who'd been stealthily watching, also from the back, took me aside during the break and said, "The County Commissioners, Vince, have assured me that if I ever wanted to reopen that pit, they'd gladly replat the road as a County Road and even take over maintenance." If true, it looked like the worm had turned and the owners were SOL. "Senator," I said,

"When we come back to order, I'll put you on the stand to bring that into evidence, if you like, and we'll call one of the Commissioners to confirm it." Reconvening, I rapped the gavel only to discover that the Senator was nowhere in sight, having apparently declined my offer. There being no more testimony, I asked if his lawyers still wanted to voir dire me, but they withdrew their motion. Hearing closed.

The record of proceedings then went back to the full Council for a decision at its next meeting. We had jurisdiction over compliance with state surface mining regulations, but the County revelations had no impact on that, nor we on their enforcement of local planning rules. In recognition of the obvious effects the pit would inflict upon its neighbors, we imposed the strictest limits we could on hours of operation, lighting, noise and dust control per the state reg's but had no basis for denying Hansen a permit to proceed. But that wasn't the rest of the story. Once the revelations about Hansen's road access problem hit the local press and public sentiment fell squarely behind the landowners, the Commissioners had little choice but to deny the needed county approval of the project. I'm sure the Senator gave them hell at their next informal chit-chat over their weekly breakfasts at the Wort Hotel coffee shop, but rules are rules. Thinking back to Don Phillips at the court-house door, I said to myself maybe the planning process wasn't such a bad idea after all.

This brief roll-back in my creeping disillusionment with planning as a world-saving tool, returns to mind two more friends in high places that you've already met, Jean and Phil Hocker. Although politically astute, they were the very antithesis of some of the politicians noted above. Unlike me, they never lost their faith in environmental activism, and their respective achievements deserve mention here. Following their Jackson Hole years, they relocated in 1987 to Washington, DC and carried the fight to the heart of the beast where their talents might have better effect.

Phil and Jean Hocker - Photo Unknown

As a result of her stewardship of the upstart Jackson Hole Land Trust, Jean had seen the power of conservation easements to permanently preserve private lands without the daunting need to purchase them outright and accept the endless burden of public management. Upon arrival in Washington, she took over as President and CEO of the then fledgling Land Trust Alliance, founded in 1982 to represent the interests of the growing Land Conservation movement in Congress. Under her leadership, both that movement and its clout in Washington increased dramatically. Today, its 1700 member-organizations, including JHLT, have protected more than 47 million acres of land nation-wide, with no end in sight. After her tenure with LTA, Jean moved on to the board of the Wilderness Land Trust, a national organization dedicated to acquiring private inholdings threatening federally protected wilderness. At present, WLT has transferred 48,000 acres into public ownership in 100 designated Wilderness Areas.

Jean's husband Phil and I go way back, having become acquainted as students at Princeton in the mid-60s, he an undergrad and me in the master's program. Sharing passions for both architecture and mountaineering, we became fast friends culminating in his arrival in Jackson to join design Associates a decade later. During his tenure there we worked together on numerous projects, collaborating at one point on a clever, but unsuccessful submission to a competition for the design of a new governor's mansion in Cheyenne. Disappointingly, the winner was an expanded version of a plain-old suburban house bearing little relation to Wyoming or the West. In our spare time, we climbed together, sharing with others a three-week crossing of British Columbia's enormous Homathko Icefield in 1977 and jointly survived being run over by an avalanche in the Tetons several years later.

Prior to their move back to Washington Phil had served six years on the Sierra Club Board of Directors and was Club Treasurer for the last four. At the time, proposed expansion of the Jackson Hole Airport was a local issue and both the Club and Phil were urging restraint. Phil nevertheless had to fly often to San Francisco and elsewhere in his duties as a Club officer. It is a measure of his dedication, that he would drive to Idaho Falls, Idaho, to catch a plane to Salt Lake for such trips despite the fact that Salt Lake flights left daily from Jackson. During that time, Phil was also instrumental in the 1984 creation of the 317,874-acre Gros Ventre Wilderness, right outside Jackson's back door. In doing so, he'd learned his way around congress, even garnering Senator Hansen's support for the bill. Once back in the capital, he founded and for a number of years directed the Mineral Policy Center. Its goal was repeal of the grossly outdated 1872 Mining Act, a virtual give-away of public land to a largely unregulated industry. As a testimony to the power of that lobby, the Act continues in effect today despite numerous hard-fought efforts at repeal. Phil's efforts nevertheless helped neutralize some of the Act's most onerous provisions. He continues the good fight as I write this, though sadly he lost Jean in 2020. I count myself lucky to count them both as friends and colleagues.

CHAPTER 10

JACKSON HOLE, 2017

Nancy and I left Jackson Hole in 1998. We were older, the winters were actually shorter, but seemed longer and we weren't skiing much anymore. We'd been there for nearly half of our lives and it was time for a change. My sons were all grown, living elsewhere and doing fine. Where to Go? Someplace warmer, but not hot. Mountains, definitely, but not snowy, or at least a lot less so. How about Mexico? We loved it there and had traveled a lot south of the border, but nothing had caught our fancy. I suggested the Four Corners, having been there a number of times with archaeological friends. I liked it a lot, but Nancy had never been there and said, "Where? In the whole world, you're talking about a place in the desert where four states come together? You've gotta be kidding?"

Then, one Easter weekend, we decided to get away from the melting slush and mud of spring in the Tetons and go have a look, planning to camp out in southeast Utah, then still an uncrowded treasure-house of deep sandstone canyons and Anasazi ruins. En route there, we spotted an apparent short cut via an unpaved road down a canyon I'd never seen before and decided to have a look. The cotton-woods were leafing out, the hayfields were greening up and the closest snow was atop a nearly ten thousand-foot mountain, looming to the south. It was gorgeous, the perfect antidote for spring in the Tetons. About halfway through, we topped a rise and an especially wonderful vista opened up onto the lush, irrigated hayfields. "Wow," Nancy said, "You know, I think I could live here!"

Our magic canyon in fall color - Photo Vincent R. Lee

She was right. It was exactly what we'd been looking for: warm, sunny and green in April with hay for the horses, a creek running through it and a handsome sometimes-snow-capped mountain standing above it all. I sent up a silent prayer of thanks to the cosmos and we cut our camping a day short to stop over in a nearby town and talk to a realtor before heading back up to Wyoming. What happened as a result doesn't have much to do with Jackson Hole, except for one thing. Our subsequent decision to sell the old Skyline Granary and surrounding eleven acres, all bought some years earlier acres at we thought at the time top dollar, nevertheless netted enough proceeds to put together a pretty spacious horse and hay outfit in the remote high desert of the Four Corners. In other words, we did what so many before us and since have done: we cashed in on the gentrification of the Last of the Old West.

Meanwhile, back to my story: August 2017 brought the path of a total solar eclipse directly over Jackson Hole and many new visitors were expected to join the already huge high-season tourist crush for the event. It was expected to be a zoo, but also literally a once-in-a-lifetime chance to view such a rare phenomenon. Since we could stay with and enjoy the show in the company of my son Chris and his family, Nancy and I decided to go despite some health issues I was dealing with at the time. Chris had been running D/A since my departure twenty years earlier and we'd been going back up every so often ever since. The local scene was therefore not a total shock, but the addition of the eclipse people brought into sharp focus the utter transformation that had taken place in the half-century since I'd first made the valley my home. We flew in with a Colorado friend and his daughter and granddaughter on his twin-engine Cessna 425 'Conquest I', a very nice seven seat aircraft. Fortunately, Tom, the owner and our pilot, had called ahead for tie-down space on the tarmac, since lots of traffic was expected. It is worth recalling that the Jackson Hole airport had long ago become the busiest in Wyoming, bringing in 767s full of summer tourists or skiers from all over the world in winter. On final approach, we saw that several were already offloading at the gates with one or two ahead of us in line for landing.

Today's even larger and busier Jackson Hole Airport - Photo Unknown

That, however, wasn't what caught our eyes. It was the flotilla of executive jets, seemingly parked on every square inch of concrete available and even out in the sagebrush beyond the tarmac. I've no idea how many; thirty, forty, maybe more. At $2.5 million a pop, the money spread out below our windows would have turned the head of Bill Gates. As we taxied to our reserved space and parked, it was as if a rowboat had docked among a flotilla of cruise ships, their Masters opulent nomads here today, gone tomorrow, and back again at their whim. It was a reflection of some simple facts. In 2014, Teton County was named "Richest County in America," with an average income of $300K and median property values of $750K. This, in a county with fewer than 25,000 residents and its only incorporated city with fewer than 10,000. Recall that they are both in a state without an income tax and you start to get the picture. Even so, "The Last and now Best of the Old West" nevertheless remains stunningly beautiful due to the largess of Nature, the federal government, fifty years of tireless work by a generation of dedicated tree-huggers and the rich able and willing to lock up big tracts as private preserves. It is even uncrowded if you stay out of town, holed up on such a preserve, and even cheap if you offset the considerable expense thereof with your giant income tax savings.

The above benefits are misleading though, if you don't happen to be rich and work in town amongst the 2.6 million tourists who invade Jackson Hole each year and the legions of service people who, unable to afford living there, commute in and out of the valley every day. Most of the skiers fly in, but summer traffic deadlocks Jackson and all three highways that meet there. Parking anywhere near where you're going is out of the question. The Town Square and environs are mobbed with crowds of out-of-town pedestrians, snapping pictures and looking for non-existent bargains. High end clothing stores, art galleries gold-plated tomahawk shops have driven most basic services to the outskirts, where K-Mart, Albertsons, Smiths and Ace Hardware have replaced the folksy mom and pop establishments of old. Pricey restaurants cluster around The Square, while chains and fast food places litter the periphery. In other words, Jackson has become a lot like everywhere else, but with faux-western store fronts, more cars, bigger crowds and a lot fewer bargains. Don't misunderstand me, it is still a nice little town off-season, home to lots of good people, some of them old friends, but it's become the victim of its own success, like tourist destinations all over the west, or for that matter, the world.

Moving out into the county, the open spaces once working cattle ranches, are either subdivisions, golf courses or fallow hay meadows set aside by conservation easements. Due to the latter, the scene remains attractive, if less than real. Bike paths flank the roadsides. Helmeted and Spandex-clad riders occasionally stop traffic where once cattle-drives occasionally held things up. Tucked tastefully into the trees, the second and third homes of the moderately wealthy are everywhere, more than a few designed by me. The Rocky Mountain mega-lodges of the truly rich are seldom seen, screened behind lots of exquisitely expensive acreage well off paths beaten by the public. A few of those are mine as well, the occasional lairs of the opulent nomads noted earlier. Among them, there's even a super-right-wing crowd imagining Jackson Hole to be Ayn Rand's mountain Shangri La where Atlas finally shrugged and told all of us 'takers' to go to hell.

As I write this, controversy grips the valley over a plan proposed by one of Jackson Hole's oldest and now wealthiest ranching families to develop yet another 100 acres of their extensive holdings in South Park. This southernmost extension of the valley, you may recall, was the scene of my long-ago five-mile ski tour with Cliff Poindexter from his place to mine during which we saw not a single building, missing in the waning daylight and falling snow the lone abandoned stone ranch house along our way. Covering nearly 7500 acres, South Park was then a gigantic hayfield, much of it owned by the family in question. Now, five decades later, it is the site of a large southern commercial appendage of Jackson, two schools and hundreds of homes scattered in ten disjointed residential subdivisions. Proposed is one more, the issue being how "affordable" the lots should be: read pricey verus less so, the county seeking 'workforce housing,' the developers, profits. At the moment, the project is stalled, but not, I suspect, for long. Absent some unlikely intervention, the rest of the south valley is just further development waiting to happen.

Wilson, site of my old post office box and now the unincorporated capital of the West Bank, has expanded and gentrified a bit, but still houses many real Jackson Holers as in the past, but now in nicely kept cottages or look-alike townhouses. The Stagecoach Bar, Nora's Fish Creek Inn and the venerable Hungry Jack's General store still cater to all of the above groups, the rich, however, mostly 'in season'. On balance, the valley remains a beautiful, pleasant place to live, certainly so for the many successful local no-longer-wannabes and the fortunate part-time refugees from urban/suburban America that can afford it. The latter new arrivals likely see it through the same rose-colored lenses that I did in 1967, but it's now a whole other place, utterly transformed from the one I knew then. Still, for newbies, it's doubtless a paradise.

Jackson, Wyo. ca 2017 with Snow King ski hill beyond -
Photo Unknown

Jackson, Wyo. ca 2017 rendered in faux logwork - Photo
Jackson Hole Traveler

But even for them, there's a downside, of course. All those happily moneyed residents need services, and that's the rub. Who's to mow the lawns, wash the dishes, make the beds, wait the tables or check out their groceries at the store. The 'business community,' an oxymoron if ever there was one, prices everything at what the traffic will bear, which is a lot, while paying their help as little as they can get away with, which is not much. New construction, my little slice of the pie, employs hundreds of the not-so-wealthy, building part-time palaces like the Frémont Mansion of my youth, driving over the hill or down the canyon twice a day to fleets of clustered doublewides no longer permitted in the valley. Their only alternative is the decidedly un-American practice of living 8 or 10 to a unit in one of the few grand-fathered trailer parks still scattered here and there around the county. This is the option favored by the sizable and growing, family-oriented Hispanic community that's sprung up in recent decades. These good people and their gringo equivalents, increasingly augmented by hip youngsters from all over the world, aren't in Jackson for the gracious living, hiking, fishing and golf, or even the scenery. They're here for the thousands of jobs needed to keep the place going. The result is a hubristic Rocky Mountain "Atlantis," home to princes, nobles, commoners and slaves, all perched atop the ticking Yellowstone super-volcano.

Thinking back on my thirty-year-plus adventure in old Davey Jackson's Hole, a flood of memories come to mind, mostly of dear friends, good people and fine times. Never once did I regret settling there or wonder if I'd chosen the right path to where my life should go. Whether creating beautiful homes for appreciative clients, introducing young people to the joys of mountaineering or opposing the juggernaut of mindless land development, I'm mostly proud of my accomplishments. But seeing it all now from a distant time and place, it begins to look different. I see things now that never occurred to me back then. Up on the black timbered mountainsides and down among the willows and cottonwoods along the Snake where friends and I once hunted deer and elk now stand scores of handsome log and stone structures, dark and empty much of the time. Out on the meadows where my crusty, hardscrabble neighbors once cut hay in the fall, fed cows from horse-drawn sleighs in winter and pulled calves in the snow and mud of April, now gala fund raisers are yearly held for worthy causes under brightly colored tents accompanied by live chamber music. Hardly realizing what I was doing, I helped bring about both of those changes.

For all my years in the valley, a war was being waged between preservationists and developers and only now does it dawn on me that I was a soldier in both armies. Nominally, both won and both lost. The boosters made money, spent it and died or, like me, sold out and left. The enviros succeeded in conserving much of the appearance of old Jackson Hole, but its "frontier" essence is long gone, having taken that very first tram ride up Rendezvous Peak. I comfort myself thinking it was all inevitable, with or without me, but still it hurts to think I was party to the last days of the magical world I saw for the first time that day long ago from atop Togwotee Pass. If the old sign is still up there, they'd better scratch out "Old" and paint in "New" to catch up with the times. If there is still an old west someplace, it's more than likely up in Montana's Big Hole or out in the Ruby Valley of Nevada, but few who know the difference will find it in Jackson Hole anymore.

This has been a story of naive good intentions and unforeseen consequences. Nobody set out to spoil Jackson Hole. Everyone wanted to save the goose that was laying the golden eggs, but almost everyone also thought there was a way to have our cake and eat it too. There wasn't. It was all nonsense. Even the hard-core developers thought they were improving things, and in their way, they did. Their detractors like me were up against irresistible forces at work in the larger world far beyond the wild peaks surrounding the valley. There was never a future in which such a prodigiously endowed place would stand still or age slowly. Given that, it's turned out pretty well. But for the efforts of Keith Becker, Verne Hughes, Jean and Phil Hocker and the host of other activists who bent the curve of history, it could have been a whole lot worse. To them, we owe a debt of thanks for deflecting the horrors that our culture inflicts left unchecked to its rapacious imperatives.

Home - Photo Unknown

Sadly, the same cannot be said of the Earth as a whole. The very idea that we might endlessly over-populate, degrade and pollute a small planet subject to indifferent forces we hardly understand and can't control, and do so without consequence, is absurd on its face. Yet we've done it or tried and continue to even now. 'Environmentalists,' a word I've come to dislike by the way, inferring that Nature is no more than the milieu within which the human drama unfolds, talk incessantly nowadays about sustainability. It's the goose and the cake all over again and it's nonsense! The last sustainable hominids on Earth were the Neanderthals, who'd be here still but that we wiped them out early in our march to dominance, before turning our sights on everything else alive on the planet. For eons, we've been running a tab and it seems the time has finally come to pay up. The Boss has sent Vito and Rocco to collect and we don't have the money.

We're about to get our legs broken, or worse, yet we keep asking for more credit. It's completely crazy! And, lest this sound like finger pointing, I'm no less a part of the problem than anyone, just as I was all those years in what I once thought pristine Jackson Hole, Wyoming.

Claude Francis Lee, Jr. - Photo Vincent R. Lee

My elder brother, Claude Francis Lee, Jr. was, hands down, the smartest person I've ever known. He died at 85 in 2018 following a long bout with Alzheimer's. As a boy, he was a whizz at anything technical. He built his own helicopter at 17, a time when there were few yet in the air. He did poorly in school, inexplicably so in view of his obvious intelligence. Though never diagnosed, he was almost certainly dyslexic, a condition barely known at the time. Reading and writing were difficult for him and much of his life was spent teaching himself both. He was a railroad brakeman, a treasure hunter, a gold prospector, a commercial seaplane pilot, an inventor and all-round decent person. He once rebuilt an entire steam railroad in the Sierras of California and despite having no formal education worked his final years at the Los Alamos National Laboratory in New Mexico. His PhD colleagues there called him a genius, and he was. Going through his papers, I discovered this, hand-written in his typically all caps block letters, spellings as written:

THE INVENTION OF THE STEAM ENGINE HAS BROUGHT ABOUT THE INDUSTRIAL REVOLUTION WHICH CARRIES US RACING DOWN A ONE WAY ROAD TOWARD THE COLLAPSE OF OUR BEAUTIFUL PLANETS ABILITY TO NUTURE AND SUSTAIN US.

THE INVENTION OF THE COMPUTER HAS BROUGHT AOUT THE WWW INTERNET WHICH, WHAT EVER ELSE, CARRIES US RACING DOWN A ONE WAY ROAD TOWARD THE COLLAPSE OF HUMANITIES ABILITY TO CONTROL THE PROLIFERATION OF INTOLERANCE, TERRORISM, HIDEOUS WEAPONS, FANATICS AND EVIL.

IT IS PANDORAS BOX. TECHNOLOGY IS THE TERMINAL DISEASE OF CIVILIZATIONS.

"A bit extreme," you say. Maybe. I once thought so. Now, I'm not so sure. According to those who pay attention to such things, we may find out before too much longer. I hope, of course, that he's wrong, but the signs aren't encouraging. As I write this, the planet is dealing with a global pandemic and possible consequent economic collapse. "Just bad luck," you say, "We'll come out OK, as we always have in the past." Again, I hope so. The problems before us are theoretically fixable, at least, as some of the world's nations have begun to demonstrate. Sadly, not ours. America has suffered triple bad luck. The above dual crises have arisen on the watch of the worst possible national leadership imaginable, led by a president that embodies our nation's darkest traits and has encouraged the same among his numerous cult-like followers. I'm confident we'll get over these challenges one way or another, but they have cast a deep shadow over the America many of us have taken for granted most our lives.

What I'm not so sure about is the all-but-ignored crisis already unfolding, for which our current troubles are merely a dress rehearsal: climate change. We've seen it coming for decades, known how to deal with it yet done nothing until recently to avoid its impacts, almost certainly doing too little too late. At this point, there is doubt that it's fixable. The time lag between cause and effect suggests that much of our fate may already be sealed. As the governor of fire-ravaged California has succinctly put it, the Earth responds to physics, chemistry and biology, always bats 1000 and always bars last. We've eaten the last of the cake and will have to soon make do with bread, if that. The goose is on her last legs and may be cooked. We've done to the Earth what I helped do to Jackson Hole, but there's no Four Corners we can decamp to. I worry especially for my lovely granddaughter, a bright, promising teenager. The world is going to change in her lifetime, a lot, and she's going to have the change with it. I never thought I'd ever say this, but I'm fearful for her future.

OTHER BOOKS BY THE AUTHOR

Sixpac Manco, Travels Among the Incas

Chanasuyu, The Ruins of Inca Vilcabamba

Forgotten Vilcabamba, Final Stronghold of the Incas

Ancient Moonshots, Megalithic Wonders from Before Technology

Archaeology in the Rough

Building BIG with Next to Nothing

Old School, A Mountain Guide's Life Before the Net

www.ingramcontent.com/pod-product-compliance
Lightning Source LLC
Chambersburg PA
CBHW021203130626
46554CB00005B/1958